A better quality of life

A strategy for sustainable development for the United Kingdom

Presented to Parliament by the Deputy Prime Minister
and Secretary of State for Environment, Transport and the Regions
by Command of Her Majesty

Cm 4345

Department of the Environment, Transport and the Regions
Eland House
Bressenden Place
London SW1E 5DU
Telephone 0171 890 3000
Internet service http://www.detr.gov.uk/

Printed in Great Britain on material containing
75% post-consumer waste and 25% ECF pulp.

FOREWORD

By the Prime Minister – The Rt Hon Tony Blair MP

The last hundred years have seen a massive increase in the wealth of this country and the well-being of its people. But focusing solely on economic growth risks ignoring the impact – both good and bad – on people and on the environment. Had we taken account of these links in our decision making, we might have reduced or avoided costs such as contaminated land or social exclusion.

Now, as we approach the next century, there is a growing realisation that real progress cannot be measured by money alone.

In our own lives, we know the value of money. We know it can bring comfort, security, and new opportunities. But we also know that money isn't everything. Feeling safe on our streets or in our homes. Enjoying our rich and diverse countryside. Knowing that a modern, dependable NHS is there when you need it. Living in strong communities. These all matter too.

But in the past, governments have seemed to forget this. Success has been measured by economic growth – GDP – alone. We have failed to see how our economy, our environment and our society are all one. And that delivering the best possible quality of life for us all means more than concentrating solely on economic growth.

That is why sustainable development is such an important part of this Government's programme. We must ensure that our economy thrives, so we can deliver the schools and hospitals we want, the jobs we need, and provide opportunities for all. But we must ensure that economic growth contributes to our quality of life, rather than degrading it. And that we can all share in the benefits.

Talking about sustainable development is not enough. We have to know what it is, to see how our policies are working on the ground. We must hold ourselves to account – as a government, but also as a country. Because the only way in which we will succeed is if we all play our part.

All this depends on devising new ways of assessing how we are doing. The indicators set out in this White Paper do this. They set traditional measures such as GDP and employment alongside innovations such as measuring the number of birds, or how healthy we are, or the fear of crime.

We now have a strategy for making sustainable development a reality. The whole of Government is committed to this, as are many businesses, groups and individuals up and down the country. Together, we can ensure that our economy, our society and our environment grow and develop in harmony.

Tony Blair

TONY BLAIR

SUMMARY

Our Strategy for sustainable development has four main aims. These are:

- social progress which recognises the needs of everyone;

- effective protection of the environment;

- prudent use of natural resources; and

- maintenance of high and stable levels of economic growth and employment.

For the UK, priorities for the future are:

- more investment in people and equipment for a competitive economy;

- reducing the level of social exclusion;

- promoting a transport system which provides choice, and also minimises environmental harm and reduces congestion;

- improving the larger towns and cities to make them better places to live and work;

- directing development and promoting agricultural practices to protect and enhance the countryside and wildlife;

- improving energy efficiency and tackling waste;

- working with others to achieve sustainable development internationally.

Government policy will take account of ten guiding principles set out in chapter 4:

- putting people at the centre;

- taking a long term perspective;

- taking account of costs and benefits;

- creating an open and supportive economic system;

- combating poverty and social exclusion;

- respecting environmental limits;

- the precautionary principle;

- using scientific knowledge;

- transparency, information, participation and access to justice;

- making the polluter pay.

We have developed a way of measuring progress by a system of 'indicators' which are explained in chapter 3. Headline indicators identify the key issues relating to quality of life. We shall publish the headline indicators every year and report on our actions and forward plans.

Chapter 5 describes measures to build sustainable development into policies and decisions, in Government and across society.

Chapter 6 looks at how to create a sustainable economy with less impact on the environment.

Chapter 7 discusses how we plan to support better communities for people to live and work in.

Chapter 8 describes the strategy to protect our environment and natural resources, both for their own sake and for the contribution they make to our economic vitality.

Sustainable development is very much an international issue and Chapter 9 deals with international co-operation.

Chapter 10 looks briefly at the progress made in the past, the priorities for the immediate future and how we shall report on the result of our actions. The Government will publish an annual review of progress, starting in 2000.

A better quality of life provides a national focus from which local and regional action can also follow. We have set a target for all local authorities to prepare local sustainable development 'Local Agenda 21' strategies by the year 2000 and hope to have sustainable development frameworks for each English region by the end of 2000.

The Government cannot do the job alone. We need to work together, forging partnerships with business, local authorities and voluntary groups. There are many initiatives where industry and local communities are already making a difference.

Everybody can help. We are investing in a major information campaign, *Are you doing your bit?*, to explain how small changes by individuals can add up to really major improvements for us all.

CONTENTS

Chapter 1

The Need for Change   8

Chapter 2

Producing a Strategy   10

Chapter 3

Progress and Priorities   13

Chapter 4

Guiding Principles and Approaches   22

Chapter 5

Sending the Right Signals   25

Chapter 6

A Sustainable Economy   31

Chapter 7

Building Sustainable Communities   50

Chapter 8

Managing the Environment and Resources   70

Chapter 9

International Co-operation and Development   88

Chapter 10

Action and Future Reporting   95

CHAPTER 1
The Need for Change

1.1   What is sustainable development? At its heart is the simple idea of ensuring **a better quality of life for everyone, now and for generations to come.** A widely-used international definition is 'development which meets the needs of the present without compromising the ability of future generations to meet their own needs'.[1]

1.2   Although the idea is simple, the task is substantial. It means meeting four objectives at the same time, in the UK and the world as a whole:

- **social progress which recognises the needs of everyone;**

- **effective protection of the environment;**

- **prudent use of natural resources; and**

- **maintenance of high and stable levels of economic growth and employment.**

1.3   Why do we need sustainable development? Because the need for development is as great as ever, but future development cannot simply follow the model of the past. This is true for the world as a whole, and for every community in this country.

1.4   The global picture is striking. A quarter of the world's people have to survive on incomes of less than US$1 a day. A fifth have no access to health care. Huge though the challenge may seem, it is becoming larger: the world's population will increase by half, another three billion people, by 2050.[2]

1.5   This country does not have problems on such a scale. But we cannot stand aside from these issues.

Global prosperity must increase, and be more widely shared. Meanwhile, in the UK, economic growth remains vital for a better quality of life: for education, healthcare and housing, to tackle poverty and social exclusion, and to improve standards of living through better goods and services.

1.6   In the past, economic activity tended to mean more pollution and wasteful use of resources. We have had to spend to clean up the mess. A damaged environment impairs quality of life and, at worst, may threaten long term economic growth – for example, as a result of climate change. And too many people have been left behind, excluded from the benefits of development but often suffering from the side-effects.

1.7   Often we have not made the most of opportunities for improvement. For example, the energy efficiency of much of our housing is poor. The result is that fuel bills and emissions of greenhouse gases are higher than they need to be, and many people cannot afford to heat their homes properly.

1.8   We have to find a new way forward. We need greater prosperity with less environmental damage. We need to improve the efficiency with which we use resources. We need thriving cities, towns and villages based on strong economies, good access to services and attractive and safe surroundings. And we need international co-operation to overcome environmental problems, to allow trade to flourish and to help the world's poorest people as we move towards a more global society.

---

1   From *Our Common Future (The Brundtland Report)* – Report of the 1987 World Commission on Environment and Development. Oxford University Press 1987. ISBN 0 19 282080 X.

2   *Eliminating world poverty: a challenge for the 21st century*. White Paper on international development. Department for International Development, November 1997. ISBN 0 10 137892 0.

SUSTAINABLE DEVELOPMENT OBJECTIVES

Social progress which recognises the needs of everyone. Everyone should share in the benefits of increased prosperity and a clean and safe environment. We have to improve access to services, tackle social exclusion, and reduce the harm to health caused by poverty, poor housing, unemployment and pollution. Our needs must not be met by treating others, including future generations and people elsewhere in the world, unfairly.

Effective protection of the environment. We must act to limit global environmental threats, such as climate change; to protect human health and safety from hazards such as poor air quality and toxic chemicals; and to protect things which people need or value, such as wildlife, landscapes and historic buildings.

Prudent use of natural resources. This does not mean denying ourselves the use of non-renewable resources like oil and gas, but we do need to make sure that we use them efficiently and that alternatives are developed to replace them in due course. Renewable resources, such as water, should be used in ways that do not endanger the resource or cause serious damage or pollution.

Maintenance of high and stable levels of economic growth and employment, so that everyone can share in high living standards and greater job opportunities. The UK is a trading nation in a rapidly changing world. For our country to prosper, our businesses must produce the high quality goods and services that consumers throughout the world want, at prices they are prepared to pay. To achieve that, we need a workforce that is equipped with the education and skills for the 21st century. And we need businesses ready to invest, and an infrastructure to support them.

A Strategy for change

1.9   This is the challenge of sustainable development. It is substantial, but we are making progress. The Government's economic policies are increasing competitiveness and preventing a return to boom and bust. It is tackling social exclusion and improving the quality of housing, health and education services. Strong environment policies are improving our air and rivers.

1.10   For the future, we need ways to achieve economic, social and environmental objectives at the same time, and consider the longer term implications of decisions. We have to spread best practice, and build on what has already been achieved. Sometimes solutions will be obvious, such as not allowing land to be contaminated so that it has to be cleaned up. In other cases, new approaches will be needed if we are to achieve economic growth in a way which minimises its impact on the environment: for example, by making more efficient use of energy and of our transport infrastructure.

1.11   This Strategy is a catalyst for that change. It identifies priority areas for action, and indicators and targets to measure progress, against which the Government will expect to be judged. It sets out action that the Government has already taken and further initiatives that are planned, and highlights what others can do. The Government will use the Strategy as a framework to guide its policies. It will encourage others to do the same.

Government looks forward to forging new partnerships on sustainable development with the devolved administrations. It hopes that this Strategy will help the devolved administrations to address their task.

The European Union

2.6   Sustainable development requires international co-operation on matters such as trade, the relief of global poverty, and environmental problems. For the UK, the European Union is especially influential. *Towards Sustainability*, the fifth Environmental Action Programme of the European Union, was adopted in 1992.[9] The Programme sought to integrate environmental concerns into other policy areas in order to achieve sustainable development.

2.7   Changes to the Treaty of Rome, agreed in the Treaty of Amsterdam, give sustainable development a much greater prominence in Europe, by making it a requirement for environmental protection concerns to be integrated into EU policies. The Treaty states that the particular objective of this requirement is to promote sustainable development. At the Cardiff European Council in June 1998, EU Member States reaffirmed their support for integration of environmental concerns into policy making, endorsing the principle that major policy proposals by the European Commission should be accompanied by appraisal of their environmental impact.

2.8   Many of the policies in this Strategy have been shaped by decisions at European level, for example on the single European market or on environmental policy.

9   *Towards Sustainability: a European Community programme of policy and action in relation to the environment and sustainable development.* Commission of the EC. Official publication of the EC, 1992. Cm (92) 23/Final/II.

SUSTAINABLE DEVELOPMENT OBJECTIVES

Social progress which recognises the needs of everyone. Everyone should share in the benefits of increased prosperity and a clean and safe environment. We have to improve access to services, tackle social exclusion, and reduce the harm to health caused by poverty, poor housing, unemployment and pollution. Our needs must not be met by treating others, including future generations and people elsewhere in the world, unfairly.

Effective protection of the environment. We must act to limit global environmental threats, such as climate change; to protect human health and safety from hazards such as poor air quality and toxic chemicals; and to protect things which people need or value, such as wildlife, landscapes and historic buildings.

Prudent use of natural resources. This does not mean denying ourselves the use of non-renewable resources like oil and gas, but we do need to make sure that we use them efficiently and that alternatives are developed to replace them in due course. Renewable resources, such as water, should be used in ways that do not endanger the resource or cause serious damage or pollution.

Maintenance of high and stable levels of economic growth and employment, so that everyone can share in high living standards and greater job opportunities. The UK is a trading nation in a rapidly changing world. For our country to prosper, our businesses must produce the high quality goods and services that consumers throughout the world want, at prices they are prepared to pay. To achieve that, we need a workforce that is equipped with the education and skills for the 21st century. And we need businesses ready to invest, and an infrastructure to support them.

A Strategy for change

1.9   This is the challenge of sustainable development. It is substantial, but we are making progress. The Government's economic policies are increasing competitiveness and preventing a return to boom and bust. It is tackling social exclusion and improving the quality of housing, health and education services. Strong environment policies are improving our air and rivers.

1.10 For the future, we need ways to achieve economic, social and environmental objectives at the same time, and consider the longer term implications of decisions. We have to spread best practice, and build on what has already been achieved. Sometimes solutions will be obvious, such as not allowing land to be contaminated so that it has to be cleaned up. In other cases, new approaches will be needed if we are to achieve economic growth in a way which minimises its impact on the environment: for example, by making more efficient use of energy and of our transport infrastructure.

1.11 This Strategy is a catalyst for that change. It identifies priority areas for action, and indicators and targets to measure progress, against which the Government will expect to be judged. It sets out action that the Government has already taken and further initiatives that are planned, and highlights what others can do. The Government will use the Strategy as a framework to guide its policies. It will encourage others to do the same.

CHAPTER 2

Producing a Strategy

2.1   In 1992, nearly 180 countries met at the 'Earth Summit' in Rio de Janeiro to discuss how to achieve sustainable development. They agreed a plan of action, *Agenda 21*,[1] and recommended that all countries should produce national sustainable development strategies. The United Kingdom was one of the first to do so, in early 1994.[2]

2.2   After coming to power in 1997, the current Government announced its intention to prepare a new Strategy. A consultation document, *Opportunities for change*, and a summary leaflet for the general public were published in February 1998.[3] Supplementary consultation documents on particular aspects of sustainable development were also produced.[4] The Government also consulted on a set of headline indicators of sustainable development (see chapter 3). The outcome of the main consultation process is summarised at the end of this chapter; further details are available.[5]

2.3   In preparing this Strategy, the Government has built on the achievements of the 1994 strategy. But a new approach is needed, which emphasises the social dimension of sustainable development alongside economic issues, the environment and resource use. This aspect of *Opportunities for change* was particularly welcomed.

Devolution

2.4   Devolution is another important change from 1994. Bringing government closer to the people through devolution is itself a policy for sustainable development: the idea of 'thinking globally, acting locally' has long been associated with sustainable development. The new devolved administrations in Scotland, Wales and Northern Ireland have the opportunity to deliver policies for sustainable development which reflect their institutions, their landscape, their culture and their way of life. While responsibility for international agreements and for matters such as taxation will remain with the UK Government, much domestic policy will be devolved:

- in Scotland, policy will be devolved to the Scottish Parliament. In February 1999, the Government published *Down to Earth*,[6] which outlines major issues of sustainable development for Scotland;

- in Wales, the National Assembly for Wales has a duty to 'make a scheme setting out how it proposes, in the exercise of its functions, to promote sustainable development'. In February 1999, the Welsh Office organised a National Conference on Sustainable Development, to discuss how this duty could be fulfilled;[7]

---

1   *Agenda 21 – Action plan for the next century*, endorsed at United Nations Conference on Environment and Development (the Earth Summit) 1992.

2   *Sustainable Development: The UK Strategy*. HMSO 1994 ISBN 0 10 124262 X.

3   *Opportunities for change*. Consultation paper on a revised UK Strategy for Sustainable Development. DETR February 1998 97EP0277.

4   *Sustainable business*. DETR, March 1998 98EP0016; *Tourism – towards sustainability*. DCMS, April 1998 JO286NJ; *Making Biodiversity Happen*. DETR, June 1998 98EP0071; *The sustainable management of forests*. Forestry Commission. July 1998 98EP02272; *Sustainable construction*. DETR, February 1998 98EP072; *Sustainability Counts*. DETR, November 1998, 98EP0492.

5   Details can be found on http://www.detr.gov.uk.

6   *Down to Earth: A Scottish Perspective on Sustainable Development*. February 1999, free from The Scottish Office, ISBN 0 7480 7171 7.

7   A report of the Welsh Office Conference is available from the Welsh Office.

• in Northern Ireland, it is anticipated that many issues relating to sustainable development will be matters for the new Assembly. In December 1998, the Government published for public comment a draft Regional Strategic Framework, *Shaping Our Future*,[8] which addresses a range of economic, social, environmental and community issues. The issues in the draft Framework are highly relevant to the delivery, through the Assembly, of sustainable development in Northern Ireland.

2.5 Where matters are devolved, the new administrations will decide how to proceed in the light of their country's particular circumstances and the needs and wishes of their people. Thus, while some of the policies described in this Strategy apply to the UK as a whole, others are exclusive to England. Reflecting this, many descriptions in this Strategy of policy initiatives in devolved areas focus on action in England, but some references are also included to parallel policies and related examples in Scotland, Wales and Northern Ireland. The UK

Opportunities for change

Over 1000 responses to *Opportunities for change* were received, ranging from local community groups to major international companies, and over 4,500 responses to the summary leaflet.

The integrated approach to sustainable development and inclusion of the social dimension were widely welcomed.

Responses to *Opportunities for change* put forward an extremely wide range of views. Those with widespread support included:

• setting challenging, measurable **targets** for each key policy area;

• highlighting **education, health and poverty** as sustainable development issues;

• government working in partnership with **business** in areas such as best practice programmes and 'market transformation';

• interest in **company** environmental or sustainable development **reporting**;

• better recognition of sustainable development in the **planning** system;

• **participation** and community empowerment as crucial to building sustainable communities;

• **transport as a key priority**, including in relation to air pollution;

• reform of **Common Fisheries** and **Common Agricultural Policies**;

• the use of **economic instruments**, provided the social aspects can be managed (e.g. impacts on low income families or on employment);

• **international co-operation** as a key to sustainable development.

Leaflet responses revealed strong concerns on transport, development, pollution and waste. Overall people wanted:

• better, cheaper **public transport** so they could use their cars less;

• less out of town development and **revitalisation of town centres** instead;

• more opportunities for **recycling**.

Regional differences in the leaflet responses were also apparent:

• Londoners were very concerned about public transport and pollution, and lack of urban green space. In contrast they were little concerned over loss of countryside to development;

• those in the south-west, north-west and eastern regions were much more concerned about the extent of development;

• those in Merseyside and Northern Ireland were particularly concerned about issues such as graffiti, litter and vandalism.

8 *Shaping Our Future. Towards a Strategy for the Development of the Region.* Draft Regional Strategic Framework. Department of the Environment (NI), December 1998. ISBN 0 337 08 376 2. Available from HMSO.

Government looks forward to forging new partnerships on sustainable development with the devolved administrations. It hopes that this Strategy will help the devolved administrations to address their task.

The European Union

2.6 Sustainable development requires international co-operation on matters such as trade, the relief of global poverty, and environmental problems. For the UK, the European Union is especially influential. *Towards Sustainability*, the fifth Environmental Action Programme of the European Union, was adopted in 1992.[9] The Programme sought to integrate environmental concerns into other policy areas in order to achieve sustainable development.

2.7 Changes to the Treaty of Rome, agreed in the Treaty of Amsterdam, give sustainable development a much greater prominence in Europe, by making it a requirement for environmental protection concerns to be integrated into EU policies. The Treaty states that the particular objective of this requirement is to promote sustainable development. At the Cardiff European Council in June 1998, EU Member States reaffirmed their support for integration of environmental concerns into policy making, endorsing the principle that major policy proposals by the European Commission should be accompanied by appraisal of their environmental impact.

2.8 Many of the policies in this Strategy have been shaped by decisions at European level, for example on the single European market or on environmental policy.

---

9 *Towards Sustainability: a European Community programme of policy and action in relation to the environment and sustainable development.* Commission of the EC. Official publication of the EC, 1992. Cm (92) 23/Final/II.

industrialised countries: in 1996 the UK invested 16% of GDP compared with, for example, 17% in France, 18% in the US and 21% in Germany.[3] Our competitiveness has suffered as a result.

3.15 **Employment** enables people to meet their needs and improve their living standards, and makes the best use of human resources. In Spring 1998, the employment rate was about 73% of people of working

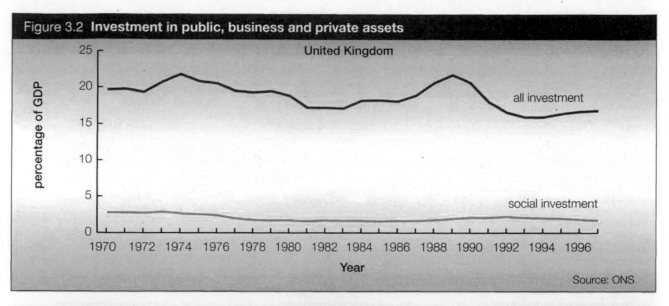

Figure 3.2 Investment in public, business and private assets

Source: ONS

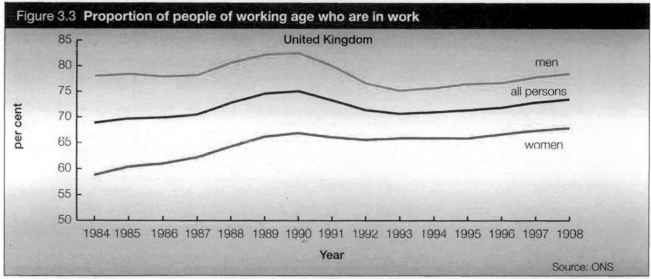

Figure 3.3 Proportion of people of working age who are in work

Source: ONS

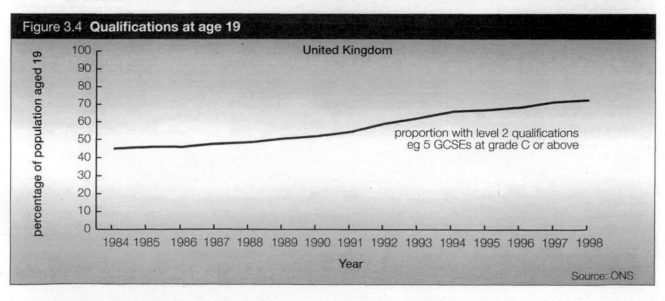

Figure 3.4 Qualifications at age 19

Source: ONS

3 OECD National Accounts Vol. 1, 1960-1996.

age. Of those out of employment, many were not looking for work and were relatively unlikely to do so, and there are still too many workless households and long term unemployed people. Providing employment opportunities for all is the single most effective means of tackling poverty and social exclusion. We have to boost skills and competitiveness to provide opportunities for the jobs which are essential to break cycles of poverty and dependence on welfare.

3.16 There has been a steady improvement in the proportion of young people gaining formal **educational qualifications**. But too many still have no formal qualifications on leaving school. Around one fifth of adults have low literacy and numeracy skills. We have to equip people with the skills to fulfil their potential in the knowledge driven society on which our future depends.

3.17 Average **life expectancy** in the UK is increasing. It compares well with most industrialised countries, although people in the UK do not live as long as those in countries such as France, Italy or Sweden.[4] And health inequalities exist: on average, men in the lowest social classes die around five years earlier than their counterparts in the highest. We have to improve the health of the population overall, and reduce health inequalities.

3.18 **Housing** is a key component of quality of life. Poor quality housing causes harm to health, and is often associated with other social problems. Most housing in the UK is in good condition but in England, for example, about 1.5 million homes are judged unfit to live in. We need to reduce the proportion of unfit stock, and improve quality overall – for example its energy efficiency and state of repair.

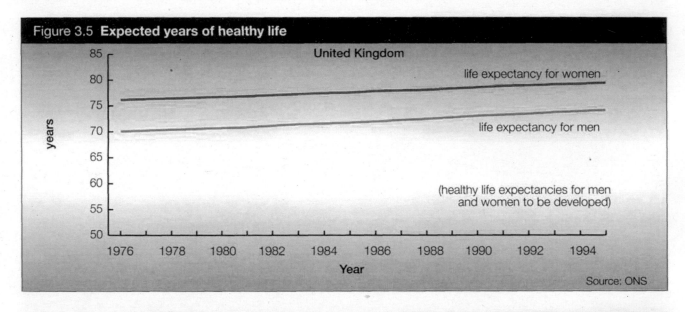

Figure 3.5 **Expected years of healthy life**

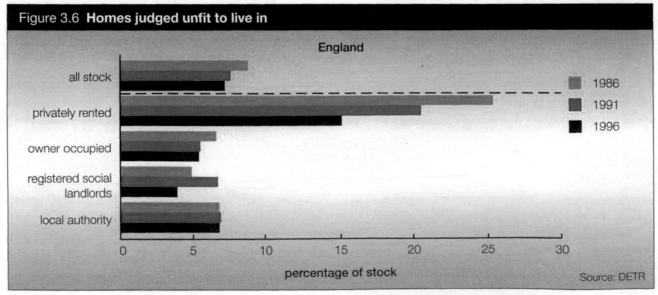

Figure 3.6 **Homes judged unfit to live in**

4 Life expectancy: comparisons with France, Italy, Sweden based on 1995 figures given in the United Nations Development Programme publication *Human Development Report 1998*.

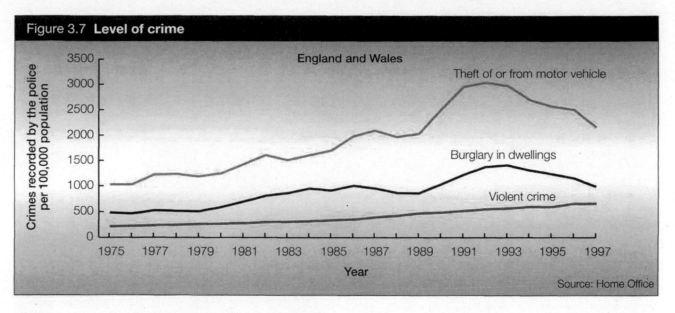

Figure 3.7 **Level of crime**

England and Wales

Theft of or from motor vehicle

Burglary in dwellings

Violent crime

Crimes recorded by the police per 100,000 population

Year

Source: Home Office

Poor quality housing causes harm to health and is often linked to other social problems

3.19 **Crime**, and fear of crime, continues to be a worry for many people. Dealing with social exclusion and environmental decline will help tackle the causes of crime, alongside measures to strengthen families and tackle drug misuse. Crime imposes economic costs, reinforces social exclusion and can hasten the environmental decline of neighbourhoods. We need to reduce both crime and people's fear of crime.

3.20 **Climate change** is one of the greatest environmental threats facing the world. In the UK, emissions of the main gases which cause climate change have fallen slightly in recent years. UK emissions of carbon dioxide (the main greenhouse gas) per head are similar to the European average and half that of the United States, and around twice the average for the world as a whole. We must continue to reduce our emissions now, and plan for greater reductions in the longer term.

3.21 We have to control **air pollution** in order to reduce risks of harm to human health and damage to the environment. On average, on more than 10% of days air pollution exceeds the no harm levels which are based on expert advice on the

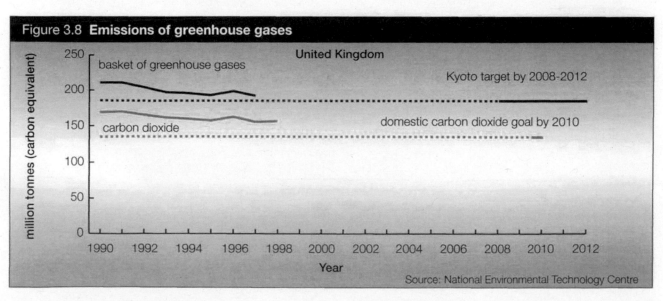

Figure 3.8 **Emissions of greenhouse gases**

United Kingdom

basket of greenhouse gases

Kyoto target by 2008-2012

carbon dioxide

domestic carbon dioxide goal by 2010

million tonnes (carbon equivalent)

Year

Source: National Environmental Technology Centre

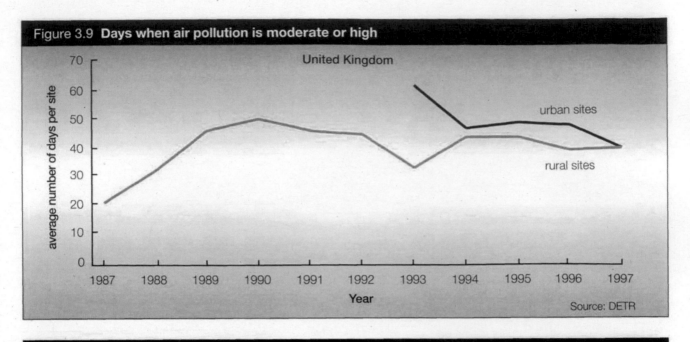

Figure 3.9 Days when air pollution is moderate or high

United Kingdom

average number of days per site

urban sites

rural sites

Year

Source: DETR

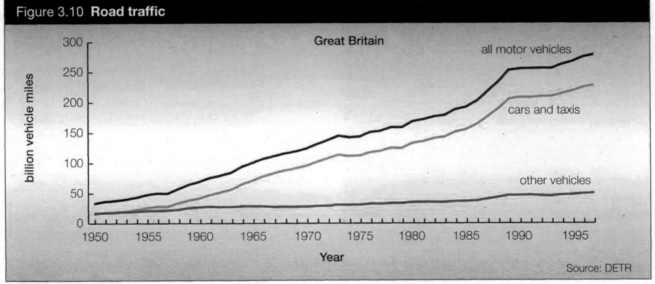

Figure 3.10 Road traffic

Great Britain

billion vehicle miles

all motor vehicles

cars and taxis

other vehicles

Year

Source: DETR

effects of air pollution on human health. This figure is too high. The Government, through its National Air Quality Strategy, has set challenging objectives to reduce air pollution and to ensure that air quality continues to improve through the longer term.

3.22 **Road traffic** has risen steadily in past decades. If no action is taken, it could increase by more than a third over the next twenty years. To prevent that, we need to meet people's needs for access and economic progress in better ways. New technologies and cleaner cars will be part of the solution, but new approaches to travel, living and working will also be needed.

3.23 Nearly 95% of **rivers** in the United Kingdom are of good or fair quality; in Scotland and Wales the proportion is even higher. There is still room for improvement; in the longer term, we must ensure that pressures such as climate change and rising

household demand for water do not lead to an overall deterioration in quality.

3.24 Populations of farmland and woodland **birds** are in long term decline, although populations of some other birds, such as open water birds, have been stable or rising. Birds are good indicators of the health of the wider environment, and we must take action to reverse these declines.

3.25 Sustainable development involves **re-using previously developed land** in order to protect the countryside and to encourage urban regeneration. The Government's target is for 60% of the additional houses in England to be built on previously developed land or provided through conversions by 2008; elsewhere in the UK the balance may be different. A large increase in households is projected to form in England over

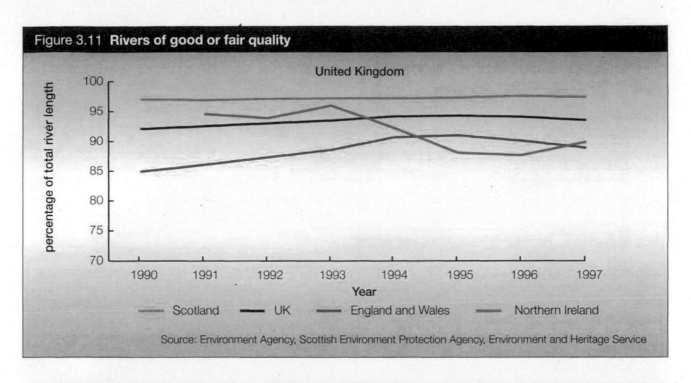

Figure 3.11 Rivers of good or fair quality

United Kingdom

— Scotland   — UK   — England and Wales   — Northern Ireland

Source: Environment Agency, Scottish Environment Protection Agency, Environment and Heritage Service

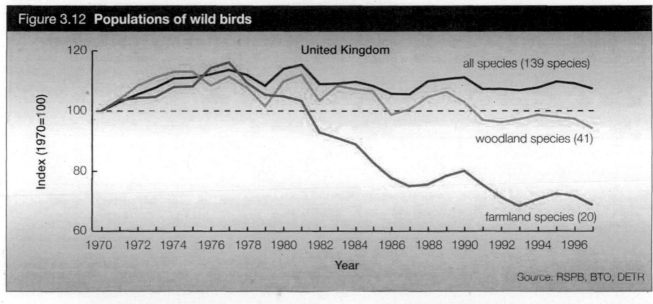

Figure 3.12 Populations of wild birds

United Kingdom

all species (139 species)

woodland species (41)

farmland species (20)

Source: RSPB, BTO, DETR

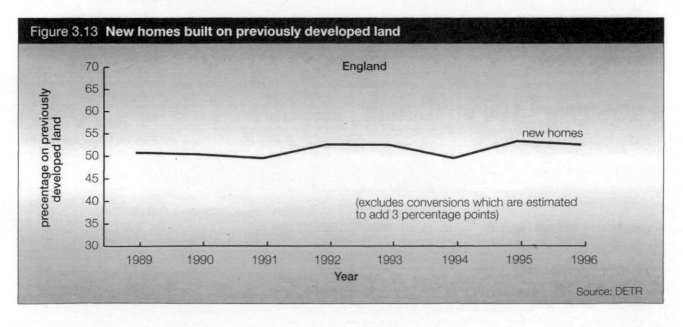

Figure 3.13 New homes built on previously developed land

England

new homes

(excludes conversions which are estimated
to add 3 percentage points)

Source: DETR

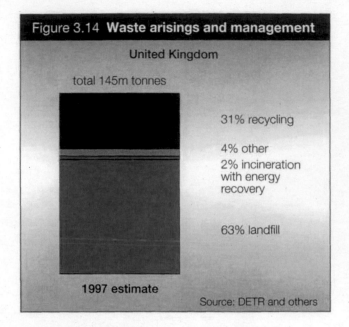

Figure 3.14 **Waste arisings and management**

United Kingdom

total 145m tonnes

31% recycling

4% other
2% incineration with energy recovery

63% landfill

1997 estimate

Source: DETR and others

the next twenty years. This means that, even with such rates of re-use, creating patterns of development that are more sustainable is a major challenge.

3.26 Households, commerce and industry in the UK produce about 145 million tonnes of **waste** a year. The amount of domestic waste, in particular, has increased steadily. While waste is only a partial measure of resource use, tackling waste is important if we are to achieve the improved resource efficiency essential for sustainable development.

3.27 The need to look at policies together, in order to make sure that by working to improve some indicators we are not worsening others, is at the heart of this Strategy. That is why, instead of looking separately at the economy, social concerns and the environment, the Strategy is organised in broad themes, looking for example at ways of building sustainable communities and delivering a sustainable economy.

The scale of the challenge

3.28 Attempts have been made to calculate the scale of the improvement in resource efficiency that will be needed to achieve sustainable development. One suggestion has been that economies could double in output while halving inputs (a so-called 'Factor 4' change) in future decades, with bigger improvements in the longer term.

3.29 In some cases, it is evident that there are limits to the amount of pollution we can create without causing unacceptable damage to human health or to the world we live in. Climate change is the most high profile current example. Substantial reductions in our consumption of fossil fuels are likely to be needed to avert catastrophic climate change. The Government's domestic goal of a 20% reduction in UK carbon dioxide emissions by 2010 recognises that the commitments agreed at Kyoto are only a first step; deeper cuts in emissions will be needed over time.

Cleaner growth: doing more with less

- global emissions of carbon dioxide amount to about 5 tonnes of carbon dioxide per person per year; the United Kingdom produces 10 tonnes per person;

- the world's population is expected to increase to around 9 billion by 2050, compared with 6 billion today; at the same time, global prosperity, particularly in developing countries, needs to increase;

- to combat the threat of climate change, significant reductions in global greenhouse gas emissions are likely to be needed: over time, emissions must therefore fall significantly beyond the targets set in the Kyoto protocol. All countries will need to play their part in this. The UK's goal of a 20% cut in its carbon dioxide emissions by 2010 can be seen as a first step in the process;

- as economies grow, significant global emissions reductions will require continually greater reductions in emissions relative to economic output, eventually rising to ten fold and beyond;

- it is not possible at this stage to forecast what reductions in UK emissions will be required, or by when. But, as an illustration, if the UK economy were to be three times larger around the middle of the next century,[5] a five fold improvement in the ratio between emissions and economic output would correspond to carbon dioxide emissions falling by 40%.

5   UK economic growth has averaged around 2¼% per year over the past 30 years. If average growth were to continue at this rate, the output of the economy would increase by over 3 times by 2050.

3.30 Similar assessments can be made in some other cases, looking at the threshold levels at which significant damage is likely – in terms of the impact of air pollution on human health, for example, or the risk to fish stocks caused by over fishing. But some important sustainable development priorities cannot be resolved in this way: for example, the rate at which greenfield land should be developed. And social progress in areas such as education, health and crime are not simply questions of resource use.

3.31 Overall, for the UK to move towards more sustainable development:

- We need more growth not less. Although, compared with many countries, the UK's economy is highly productive and our average incomes are high, we have steadily been overtaken by other nations in both respects.

- That growth must be of a higher quality than in the past. It needs to be achieved while reducing pollution and use of resources.

- Prosperity must be shared more widely and fairly: some parts of the country and some groups are falling too far behind.

- Our towns and countryside contribute significantly to our quality of life. We need to make our towns and cities better places to live and work, and to retain the special characteristics of our landscape which we most value.

- We must contribute to global sustainable development, in particular for those in extreme poverty.

Headline Indicators
Total output of the economy (GDP)
Investment in public, business and private assests
Proportion of people of working age who are in work
Qualifications at age 19
Expected years of healthy life
Homes judged unfit to live in
Level of crime
Emissions of greenhouse gases
Days when air pollution is moderate or high
Road traffic
Rivers of good or fair quality
Populations of wild birds
New homes built on previously developed land
Waste arisings and management
Other Indicator
Satisfaction with quality of life (to be developed)

CHAPTER 4
Guiding Principles and Approaches

4.1   This Strategy concentrates on setting key objectives, supported by indicators and targets. The Government's policies will also take account of ten principles and approaches which reflect key themes from the *Rio Declaration on Environment and Development*,[1] the 1994 strategy, and responses to *Opportunities for change*. Some are established legal principles.[2] Others might better be described as 'approaches' to decision making.

- **Putting people at the centre.** Sustainable development must enable people to enjoy a better quality of life, now and in the future. In the words of the *Rio Declaration*, 'human beings are at the centre of concerns for sustainable development. They are entitled to a healthy and productive life in harmony with nature.'

Sustainable development puts people at the centre

- **Taking a long term perspective.** Sustainable development thinking cannot restrict itself to the life of a Parliament, or the next decade. Radical improvements have to begin now to safeguard the interests of future generations. At the same time we must meet today's needs – for example, people need warm homes, which, at present, means using predominantly fossil fuels.

- **Taking account of costs and benefits.** Decisions must take account of a wide range of costs and benefits, including those which cannot easily be valued in money terms. In pursuing any single objective, we should not impose disproportionate costs elsewhere. Public values, the timing of costs and benefits and risks and uncertainties should be taken into account.

- **Creating an open and supportive economic system.** Sustainable development requires a global economic system which supports economic growth in all countries. We need to create conditions in which trade can flourish and competitiveness can act as a stimulus for growth and greater resource efficiency.

- **Combating poverty and social exclusion.** Eradicating poverty is indispensable for sustainable development. We must help developing countries to tackle widespread abject poverty. In this country, everyone should have the opportunity to fulfil their potential, through access to high quality public services, education and employment opportunities, decent housing and good local environments.

- **Respecting environmental limits.** Serious or irreversible damage to some aspects of the environment and resources would pose a severe threat to global society. Examples are major climate change, overuse of freshwater resources, or collapse of globally significant fish stocks. In these cases, there are likely to be limits which should not be breached. Defining such limits is difficult, so precautionary action needs to be considered.

1   *Rio Declaration on Environment and Development,* made at UNCED 1992. ISBN 9 21 100509 4.

2   e.g. see Article 174 of the Treaty establishing the European Community.

- **The precautionary principle.** The *Rio Declaration* defines the precautionary principle as 'where there are threats of serious or irreversible damage, lack of full scientific certainty shall not be used as a reason for postponing cost-effective measures to prevent environmental degradation'. Precautionary action requires assessment of the costs and benefits of action, and transparency in decision-making.

- **Using scientific knowledge.** When taking decisions, it is important to anticipate early on where scientific advice or research is needed, and to identify sources of information of high calibre. Where possible, evidence should be reviewed from a wide-ranging set of viewpoints.

- **Transparency, information, participation and access to justice.** Opportunities for access to information, participation in decision-making, and access to justice should be available to all.

- **Making the polluter pay.** Much environmental pollution, resource depletion and social cost occurs because those responsible are not those who bear the consequence. If the polluter, or ultimately the consumer, is made to pay for those costs, that gives incentives to reduce harm, and means that costs do not fall on society at large. At the same time, it may not always be possible for everyone to bear all such costs, particularly for essential goods and services.

ECONOMIC, SOCIAL AND ENVIRONMENTAL CAPITAL

4.2   These principles and approaches give full weight to economic, social and environmental aspects of sustainable development. Sometimes discussion of sustainable development, particularly in richer countries, has focused mainly on environmental limits. But economic and social boundaries must also be recognised. An economy in long term recession is not sustainable. Nor is a situation where many people are denied opportunity and face poverty and exclusion. Development which ignores the essential needs of the poorest people, whether in this country or abroad, is not sustainable development at all.

Applying the precautionary principle

The precautionary principle means that it is not acceptable just to say "we can't be sure that serious damage will happen, so we'll do nothing to prevent it". Precaution is not just relevant to environmental damage – for example, chemicals which may affect wildlife may also affect human health.

At the same time, precautionary action must be based on objective assessments of the costs and benefits of action. The principle does not mean that we only permit activities if we are sure that serious harm will not arise, or there is proof that the benefits outweigh all possible risks. That would severely hinder progress towards improvements in the quality of life.

There are no hard and fast rules on when to take action: each case has to be considered carefully. We may decide that a particular risk is so serious that it is not worth living with. In other cases society will be prepared to live with a risk because of other benefits it brings. Transparency is essential: difficult decisions on precautionary action are most likely where there is reason to think there may be a significant threat, but evidence for its existence is as yet lacking or inconclusive. Decisions should be reviewed to reflect better understanding of risk as more evidence becomes available.

The Government has taken action in areas such as air, marine and freshwater pollution where an insufficiently precautionary approach has been taken in the past. It is also committed to acting proportionately. It is working to develop a more consistent approach to the principle across Government and will report on this work in forthcoming reports on this Strategy.

4.3   We are all familiar with the idea of **economic** capital, and the need to conserve it. Families save money for a rainy day; businesses invest in order to expand and flourish; local and central governments lead the way in investing in schools, hospitals and roads.

4.4   Our **social** capital consists of the skills and knowledge, health, self-esteem and social networks of people and communities in the UK. The failure of urban renovation schemes of the recent past, which concentrated on physical investment alone – for example some 1960s and 1970s housing estates – demonstrate the importance of building social capital as well as bricks and mortar.

4.5   **Environmental** capital provides the third side of the triangle. We cannot protect every bit of the environment for ever: in some cases, individual development decisions will require trade-offs between economic, social and environmental objectives. But it is important to seek opportunities to achieve objectives simultaneously, and to consider the cumulative impact of decisions on overall environmental capital. The Government aims to prevent further overall deterioration, and to secure enhancements which contribute to an overall improvement in quality of life. That means environmental indicators in this Strategy moving in the right direction, alongside those on economic and social objectives.

4.6   Throughout this Strategy, the emphasis is on developing our economic and social capital while exercising sound stewardship over our environmental capital. That approach will underpin the Government's policies for sustainable development, and the way in which it applies the principles and approaches described above. It will commend this approach to others, including its own sustainable development advisory bodies (see chapter 5).

CHAPTER 5
Sending the Right Signals

5.1   To make sustainable development a reality, it must be built into policies and decisions. This Strategy sets a broad framework to help that happen. But we also need specific measures to drive change, both at home and abroad.

Better decision-making

5.2   The Government is putting **sustainable development at the heart of every Government Department's work:**

- it has created a powerful Cabinet Committee on the Environment, which co-ordinates policy on sustainable development;

- it has revitalised the system of 'Green Ministers'. Their job is to oversee systems for integrating the environment into each Department's policies and operations. In May 1998, they agreed a framework from which Departments have drawn up their own strategies for improving environmental performance; the introduction of environmental management systems across Government will help further improve performance;

- it has created an inter-Departmental group on international development to promote consistency on issues relevant to developing countries.

5.3   Following a commitment in the 1997 Labour Party Manifesto, the House of Commons established an Environmental Audit Committee to consider how policies and programmes of Government Departments and non-departmental public bodies contribute to environmental protection and sustainable development. The Government particularly welcomes the Committee's emerging practice of returning to topics to assess progress, and to identify where weaknesses still exist.

5.4   In future, whenever the Government creates a public body, it will consider whether to include sustainable development in its remit. It is reviewing the scope for including sustainable development as an objective of existing Departments and public bodies.

5.5   There are already **appraisal systems** which look separately at the economic, environmental, health, transport, regulatory and equal opportunities aspects of policies. The Government has strengthened mechanisms for environmental appraisal, including new policy guidance for Government Departments.[1] It is committed to a better understanding of the impacts of policies on different groups in society, particularly women, ethnic minorities, and the disabled and ensuring that findings are taken into account in policy making.[2]

Road Proposals – new approach to appraisal

The Government has developed a new approach to the appraisal of road scheme proposals. Schemes, and other projects, are assessed against criteria of environmental impact; safety; economy; accessibility (to public transport services, for example); and integration with land use and other transport proposals and polices. This approach allows options for solving transport problems to be compared and decisions taken in the light of environmental, social and economic impacts. The new approach has been developed in consultation with English Nature, English Heritage, the Environment Agency and the former Countryside Commission (now Countryside Agency). Development is continuing so that it can be applied to other modes of transport.

1   *Policy Appraisal and the Environment* April 1998. DETR 97EP0442

2   *Policy Appraisal for Equal Treatment Guidelines* – issued jointly by Home Office DFEE and Cabinet Office, November 1998.

5.6   For sustainable development to be achieved, economic, social and environmental impacts need to be considered together when policies are being devised or reviewed. The *Modernising Government* White Paper commits the Government to produce and deliver an integrated system of impact assessment and appraisal tools in support of sustainable development, covering impacts on business, the environment, health and the needs of particular groups in society.[3]

The Women's Unit

In the past, women's views were often under-represented in policy making. The Minister for Women and the Women's Unit in the Cabinet Office now help to promote women's interests, and to communicate their concerns and insights. Many sustainable development issues are of particular concern to women – such as availability and safety of public transport, accessibility of facilities to parents with young children, and environmental health.

Taxes, regulation and other policy instruments

5.7   The Government will explore the scope for using **economic instruments**, such as taxes and charges, to deliver more sustainable development. Such measures can promote change, innovation and efficiency, and higher environmental standards. They are a way to put the 'polluter pays' principle into practice, although care is needed to consider the impact on competitiveness and the social consequences: for example, ensuring that the price of essential goods like fuel or water does not lead to hardship for the least well-off.

5.8   Over time, the Government will aim to reform the tax system in ways which deliver a more dynamic economy and a cleaner environment: shifting taxes from 'goods' like employment, towards 'bads' such as pollution. It will consider carefully how revenues from taxes are used, although there are no firm rules.[4] The 1999 Budget included the biggest ever package of tax reforms to protect the environment.

Economic instruments for sustainable development

The Government has taken several measures to secure more sustainable development through economic instruments, including:

- a fuel duty differential in favour of 'ultra-low sulphur diesel'. As a result, this significantly cleaner fuel should account for almost all diesel sold in the UK by the end of 1999;

- a commitment to increase duty on petrol and diesel each year by 6% above inflation to reduce carbon dioxide emissions from road transport, 1% higher than the previous Government's commitment;

- a levy will be introduced on business use of energy in 2001, after further consultation with industry. It will be introduced on a revenue neutral basis, with offsetting cuts in employers' national insurance contributions. £50 million of support will also be provided to encourage business to invest in new environmental technologies and renewable fuels. The Government intends to set lower rates of tax for those energy intensive sectors agreeing targets for improvements in energy efficiency which meet the Government's criteria;

- a long term, revenue neutral reform of company car taxation to remove the incentive to drive additional business miles, and encourage the take up of more fuel efficient vehicles;

- from June 1999, a reduction in Vehicle Excise Duty to £100 for cars with the smallest engine sizes;

- the standard rate of landfill tax was increased to £10 per tonne from April 1999, and will further increase by £1 per tonne each year for at least the next five years.

3   *Modernising Government.* March 1999, Cm 4310. ISBN 0 10 143102 3.

4   *Environmental Taxation – Statement of Intent.* HM Treasury Press Office, 2 July 1997.

5.9   **Subsidies**, including tax relief, also have a role in some circumstances: for example, the 1999 Budget increased funding for the Government's rural transport fund to £120 million for the next two years, to extend the range of public transport services in rural communities. But care is needed not to subsidise changes which would have happened anyway. The Government will aim to avoid 'perverse subsidies' which, in promoting one objective, work against sustainable development overall. Future reporting on the strategy will include measures taken on environmental taxes and subsidies.

5.10   Where new regulation is used, it will conform to the Government's principles of better regulation, so that it is targeted at the problem in hand; clear and simple to understand; applied consistently, proportionate to the problem and the circumstances of individual businesses, voluntary groups and others; and enforced effectively and constructively by a body accountable for its conduct.[5] Those regulated need flexibility to find reliable, cost-effective ways to comply.

5.11   The Government will continue to consider the scope for voluntary agreements with industry. It has, for example, asked the aggregates industry to deliver an improved package of voluntary measures which address the significant environmental costs of aggregate extraction. If the industry is unable to deliver, then an aggregates tax will be imposed.

5.12   Which instrument is appropriate has to be determined on a case by case basis, taking account of economic, social and environmental consequences. The Government, for example, has decided not to proceed with a national tax or charges on water pollution since research has shown that this may not be the most effective way of securing targeted improvements in water quality. Often the best solution will be to mix instruments.

5.13   Where the aim of policy instruments is to limit pollution, it may sometimes be necessary for those producing the pollution to incur higher expenditure on abatement equipment. In the long term, however, the aim should be to move to cleaner processes, rather than adding on clean-up equipment. The new set of sustainable development indicators includes an indicator of expenditure on pollution abatement. Increases in such expenditure are not, in themselves, a sign of sustainable development. But such an indicator, if taken in context with other indicators, can help to show up unsustainable trends: for example, if abatement expenditure and pollution both continued to rise.

Mixing instruments for better outcomes

- household energy efficiency and fuel poverty aims are secured by grants for energy saving investment and by information campaigns. A reduced VAT rate on energy saving materials under grant schemes for the less well-off was introduced in July 1998; the Government has asked the European Commission to consider changes to EU law to allow a reduced rate on energy saving materials in other circumstances.

- reducing the proportion of waste going to landfill involves regulation on landfill site design and operation; the landfill tax; and promotion of alternative means of waste management, such as recycling.

Information and involvement

5.14   Improved awareness of sustainable development can be a powerful tool for change. In March 1998, the Government launched *Are you doing your bit?*, a campaign in England which focuses on specific issues related to sustainable development and shows people how they can influence their local and global environment. Early themes covered climate change and energy efficiency, transport and air quality. In 1999, it will extend to packaging, waste and water conservation, and links between transport and health. The Government will work with public bodies, voluntary organisations, business and trade unions to reinforce the campaign's messages.

5.15   In 1998, the Government set up the **Sustainable Development Education Panel**, whose

---

5   *The Better Regulation Guide.* Cabinet Office, Regulatory Impact Unit, August 1998.

Every day there are ten million empty seats on the road.

An advertisement from the DETR campaign *Are you doing your bit?*

remit covers schools, further and higher education bodies, and education in work, recreation and the home. The Panel's first Annual Report sets goals for the next ten years, and makes recommendations to a wide range of stakeholders.[6] The Government will respond to the Report later in 1999. The Panel has made recommendations on sustainable development education to the National Curriculum review, setting out what children should know about sustainable development by the ages of 7, 11, 14 and 16. Consultation on the revised National Curriculum will take place later in 1999, before its formal introduction in 2000.

The Children's Parliament on the Environment

The Government launched this competition for 10–11 year old schoolchildren in 1998 as an opportunity for schools to develop children's understanding of sustainable development and the democratic process. Children from 3,500 schools registered to take part in the competition which involved essay writing and debating competitions. Six winners from each region will take part in the Children's Parliament in May. The children will be able to question Government Ministers and present their action plan to the Prime Minister.

5.16 Many responses to *Opportunities for change* wanted the media, in particular television, to give sustainable development a higher profile. The Government will aim to help: for example, through information on the headline indicators and awareness raising through *Are you doing your bit?*.

5.17 The Government will continue to consult widely on policies related to sustainable development. It will consider the potential of methods highlighted in the Royal Commission on Environmental Pollution's 1998 report on *Setting Environmental Standards*:[7] for example, consensus conferences and citizens juries. It has set up the People's Panel, which consists of 5,000 people selected at random from across the country, to seek views on how to improve public services.

5.18 The Government's proposed Freedom of Information Act will mean new rights to information, including improved rights to environmental information.[8] To provide better information on industrial processes and the substances they release to the environment, the Government is developing, through the Environment Agency, a new pollution inventory to replace the current Chemical Release Inventory.

Research and advice

5.19 Research, analysis and innovation are fundamental for long term change. Much takes place in the private sector; and the Government will continue to encourage this through schemes to support research and development and the spread of best practice and networking. More generally, the Comprehensive Spending Review[9] delivered an additional £1.4 billion over three years in funding for science.

5.20 The Government has made sustainable development an underpinning theme of its Foresight programme.[10] Foresight aims to promote wealth creation and better quality of life by looking

6   *Sustainable Development Education Panel: First Annual Report, 1998*. DETR C8551. 98EP0585

7   *Setting environmental standards*. Royal Commission on Environmental Pollution: Cm 4053, October 1998. ISBN 0 10 140532 4.

8   The Act will implement provisions on environmental information in the Aarhus Convention on Access to Information, Public Participation in Decision-Making and Access to Justice in Environmental Matters, signed by the United Kingdom in 1998.

9   *Modern Public Services for Britain: Investing in Reform*. Comprehensive Spending Review: New Public Spending Plans 1999-2002 July 1998 ISBN 0 10 1401124.

10 Information on the Foresight programme from http://www.foresight.gov.uk/, or Office of Science and Technology.

Research and innovation are essential for change

at future needs, opportunities and threats, and how developments in science could help the UK to meet these challenges.

5.21 The next stage of Foresight will consider the ageing population, manufacturing changes in the next twenty years, and crime prevention, as well as important sectors: the built environment and transport; chemicals; defence and aerospace; energy and the natural environment; financial services; the food chain and industrial crops; healthcare; information, communications and media; materials; and retail and consumer services.

Preparing for an ageing population

The increasing age of the population will affect many aspects of sustainable development. The Foresight programme will be looking at issues such as healthcare provision, transport, and retail, consumer and financial services specifically from the perspective of the needs of an ageing population.

5.22 An increasing amount of Government support through the Research Councils has sustainable development as a theme. Physical and biological sciences, engineering, economics and social sciences are all relevant. For example:

- the Economic and Social Research Council is launching a new programme on 'Delivering Sustainability';

- the Engineering and Physical Sciences Research Council has current or planned programmes on sustainable cities, waste minimisation, integrated transport and sustainable manufacturing.

5.23 The Government aims to improve the public's understanding of science and to secure public confidence in how the Government uses the best available scientific advice in decision making. Implementation of the Chief Scientific Adviser's guidelines on the use of scientific advice in policy making is an important part of this work.[11] These guidelines expand on the key considerations for using scientific knowledge outlined in chapter 4.

ADVISORY BODIES

5.24 The 1994 strategy created the British Government Panel on Sustainable Development and the UK Round Table on Sustainable Development. The Panel advises on major strategic issues for sustainable development. The Round Table consists of people drawn from a variety of organisations and interests and seeks to build consensus about ways of achieving sustainable development.

5.25 To help take forward this Strategy and to provide a focal point for considering sustainable development in this country, the Government proposes to establish, from the beginning of 2000, a new Sustainable Development Commission. This will subsume the Panel and the Round Table. The Commission's main responsibility will be to monitor progress on sustainable development, and to build consensus on action to be taken by all sectors to accelerate its achievement. The Government will be discussing further with the Panel, the Round Table and other interested groups the precise remit and working methods for the Commission.

5.26 The Government will continue to look to the Advisory Committee on Business and the Environment and the Trades Union and Sustainable Development Advisory Committee to provide strategic advice on issues which are of major concern to business and to employees. It will

11 *The Use of Scientific Advice in Policy Making.* A note by the Chief Scientific Adviser, Sir Robert May (1997). Office of Science and Technology, DTI Publications 3040/0.5k/10/97/RP.

support those bodies in generating leadership on sustainable development issues and their application in all aspects of business practice and in the workplace.

5.27 The Government will continue to work with the Royal Commission on Environmental Pollution to identify priority areas for its advice.

Key actions and commitments

- Creation of all new public bodies to include consideration of specific remit on sustainable development

- Integrated appraisal system in support of sustainable development

- Taking better account of needs of women, through the work of Women's Unit

- Further use of economic instruments for sustainable development, including new energy levy

- Reinforced public awareness campaign, *Are you doing your bit?*

- Improved rights to environmental information

- New Sustainable Development Commission

- Sustainable development as a key theme of new Foresight programme

Indicators

Green housekeeping in Government

Women in public appointments and in senior positions

Prices of key resources (e.g. fuel, water)

Real changes in the cost of transport

Enforcement of regulations (to be developed)

Public understanding and awareness

Individual action for sustainable development

Awareness in schools (to be developed)

Expenditure on pollution abatement

CHAPTER 6

A Sustainable Economy

To deliver a more sustainable economy we need:

- to do more with less: making better use of resources;

- a stable and competitive economy;

- to develop skills and reward work;

- goods and services which meet consumers' needs and are produced, and can be used, ever more efficiently;

- Government, producers and consumers working together to achieve long term change.

6.1   A better quality of life for all will require better, more widely available goods and services: decent housing, efficient household equipment; safe and nutritious food; and access to a growing range of leisure activities. We have to meet those needs in ways which deliver overall sustainable development objectives on social progress, the environment, resource use, and economic growth and employment.

6.2   To do so requires a stable and competitive economy. We must continue to increase productivity and the efficiency with which we use resources. And goods and services must be produced in ways that treat people fairly, give them the opportunity to fulfil their potential and make the best use of their skills and knowledge.

6.3   The links between these objectives are clear. Social, environmental and resource issues are increasingly strategic issues for business: growth based on environmental damage, or unfairness and division in society, is not sustainable. Continued improvements in resource efficiency are essential

for the UK's future prosperity and competitiveness, as well as the health of the environment. Business needs a strong, stable economy as the basis for innovation and investment, on which future jobs depend.

6.4   The Government's role is to set a framework of policies to enable business to respond to these challenges, to help consumers influence change, and give people the opportunity to develop skills and secure employment.

Doing more with less: improving resource efficiency

6.5   Greater resource efficiency is a key to change. Often it is the environmental impacts of resource use which are of most concern. Fossil fuel use is already causing climate change; we are producing volumes of waste which can be expensive and increasingly difficult to dispose of and generating more traffic than roads and many communities can cope with.

6.6   Thirty years ago, there was speculation about the world running out of natural resources, especially non-renewable resources such as oil. Since then, the immediate threat has appeared to recede, though we must still have an eye to the long term availability of resources for the growing world population and for future generations. Over the last few years, however, we have realised that a more urgent threat arises from the environmental damage caused by the extraction, use and disposal of natural resources. And we now understand that sustainable development also means making sure that the rate of consumption of renewable resources does not reduce their availability for future generations.

6.7   Just to keep the UK's resource use at today's levels would require resource efficiency to improve at a rate which matches the growth in the economy. But that rate of change will not be enough to reduce global environmental pressures which are already severe, in particular since increases in global consumption will be necessary to eradicate extreme poverty. The place of poverty eradication and sustainable consumption and production patterns as overarching issues for the United Nations Commission on Sustainable Development reflects their importance and the links between them.

6.8   Progress has been made in many areas. For example, washing powders are less bulky, do not need such hot water, and get clothes cleaner. New production processes have reduced serious pollution, often bringing down costs and resource use. But the amount of goods and services has grown, and the way in which they are used has changed. For example:

- many UK homes now have two or more television sets, often left on standby, which increases their electricity use by around a quarter – and over 22 weeks, consumes more energy than was used in making them;

- for road transport, the number of miles we travel for every gallon of fuel has changed little over many years, even though engines are generally more fuel-efficient. More journeys are now made by car, rather than public transport, and extra safety features and tougher emissions controls have sometimes increased fuel consumption.

Each household produces an average of over one tonne of waste per year

6.9   In the case of energy, the net result has been that overall consumption in the UK has been roughly stable since 1970, while the economy has grown by over 80%. The energy intensity of manufacturing industry has fallen by rather more than that of the economy as a whole. Average energy consumption per household has hardly improved at all.

6.10   **A faster rate of change will be needed in future.** Past rates of change do not limit what is achievable, since they reflect a time when sustainable development was not recognised as a core issue. Future progress will involve better production processes and delivering what consumers want in

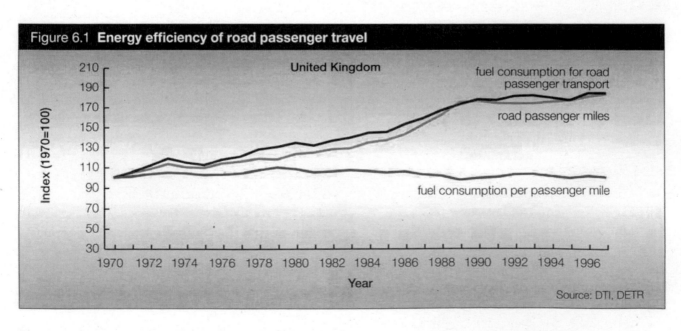

Figure 6.1 **Energy efficiency of road passenger travel**

United Kingdom

fuel consumption for road passenger transport

road passenger miles

fuel consumption per passenger mile

Index (1970=100)

Year

Source: DTI, DETR

new ways. Some sectors of the economy will be able to do more than others: many goods and services that will be important in 2050 have yet to be invented. Innovations such as the fuel cell are developing faster than seemed likely even very recently.

6.11 Chapter 3 shows that, over the next fifty years and beyond, significant cuts in UK carbon dioxide emissions are likely to be required alongside economic growth. We cannot predict the exact extent of change, but as the illustrative figures in the box after paragraph 3.29 show, the ratio between emissions and economic output may ultimately have to change many-fold. That will mean major changes in the way we produce and use energy.

Waste

Waste is a reflection of the amount of goods and services consumed and the efficiency of resource use. In the UK we produce around 400 million tonnes of solid and sludge waste each year, of which it is estimated around 145 million tonnes comes from industry, commerce and households. Each household produces, on average, over one tonne each year.

The draft waste strategy for England and Wales will be published shortly. It will set out policies for sustainable waste management in the period to 2020. It will set targets with the aim of moving away from disposal, which makes the least use of waste, towards waste minimisation, reuse, recycling and recovery. Similar strategies are being produced for Scotland and Northern Ireland.

6.12 For other resources, the scale of the challenge will vary. Predictions can be unreliable, as previous estimates of resource availability have shown. In consequence, the Government does not propose to set a specific 'resource efficiency' target for the UK. The order of change that could be required by the middle of next century, or how it might be achieved, remains uncertain. But the scale of the

overall challenge to improve resource efficiency may be as significant as for carbon dioxide emissions. That can help thinking about how, in the long term, goods and services need to be delivered in more innovative and resource-efficient ways. Measures referred to elsewhere in this Strategy – for example to promote more efficient production and transport – will help in moving towards this goal.

6.13 Reliable methods of assessing resource efficiency are still being developed. For the moment, the headline indicator on waste will help to show progress. Reports on this Strategy will also include an indicator on energy efficiency of the economy. The Government will develop further new indicators and include them in future reports.

Key actions and commitments

- Promote continual improvements in resource efficiency
- Draft waste strategies will be published shortly

Indicators

Waste arisings and management (headline)

UK resource use (to be developed)

Waste by sector (to be developed)

Household waste and recycling

Materials recycling

Energy efficiency of economy

Energy use per household

Hazardous waste

ECONOMIC STABILITY AND COMPETITIVENESS

6.14 Over the past three decades UK output and inflation has been highly volatile. Economic instability has significant costs. It makes it hard for individuals and firms to plan and invest, damaging long-term economic growth. It involves social costs that often fall heavily on people on lower incomes.

6.15 In 1997 the Government inherited an economy that was showing signs of repeating the pattern of boom and bust: demand was growing much faster than growth in the economy's productive capacity; inflationary pressures were increasing; and public finances were in significant structural deficit.

6.16 In response, the Government moved quickly to put in place a framework to deliver a stable economic environment, now and in the future:

- the monetary policy framework has been reformed to deliver low inflation. The Bank of England now sets interest rates to meet the Government's inflation target of keeping the annual increase in the Retail Price Index (excluding mortgage interest payments) at 2.5%;

- the Government has introduced the Code for Fiscal Stability and specified two strict fiscal rules: the 'golden rule' and the 'sustainable investment rule'. These require that, over the economic cycle, the Government borrows only for investment, and not consumption, and that the level of borrowing must be consistent with keeping public sector net debt, as a proportion of GDP, at a stable and prudent level.

6.17 The rewards from the new framework are already evident. Inflation is close to target and expected to remain so, while long-term interest rates are at their lowest level for over 40 years. The structural fiscal deficit has been eliminated and both fiscal rules are on track to be met over the economic cycle. As a result, the economic cycle is projected to be much more moderate than in the past.

Stability and investment for the long term

The Government reviewed its spending programmes – current and capital – in the Comprehensive Spending Review, completed in July 1998. This set out plans for overall spending over the remainder of this Parliament, based on the fiscal rules and the Government's key spending priorities. Within that framework, the Government announced:

- an extra £19 billion for education, underpinning the drive to raise standards;

- an extra £20 billion for modernisation of health services;

- an extra £1.7 billion to improve public transport and modernise the road and rail network;

- an extra £3.9 billion of investment in housing and £800 million for the New Deal for Communities, promoting regeneration of our cities and combating social exclusion;

- substantial investment in crime prevention.

In addition, the Investing in Britain Fund was created to provide for renewal and reform of infrastructure and the public sector. Public sector net investment will double over the life of the current Parliament, while remaining well within the limits of the fiscal rules.

6.18 By 1997, the labour productivity gap between the UK and major competitors[1] was around 40% compared to the United States and around 20% compared to France and Germany. In the White Paper, *Our Competitive Future*,[2] and in the 1999 Budget,[3] the Government outlined initiatives to promote UK competitiveness in a knowledge driven world. These include:

- increased support for new businesses and new technology, including a new advice service

---

1 Labour productivity gap based on GDP per worker.

2 *Our Competitive Future: building a knowledge based economy.* December 1998, Cm 4176. ISBN 0 10 14762 4.

3 *Steering a stable course for lasting prosperity: pre-budget report*, November 1998, Cm 4076. ISBN 0 10 140762 9.

targeting 10,000 start-ups a year in England, investment in science (see chapter 5), and measures to promote commercialisation of university research;

- measures to promote collaboration between companies and within regions, including through the new Regional Development Agencies;

- backing the Confederation of British Industry's *Fit for the Future* initiative to encourage a massive increase in take up of best practice;

- promoting small business investment and growth through changes in corporation tax and capital allowances and a new research and development tax credit.

Competitiveness Index

The Competitiveness White Paper announced that the Government will develop a set of competitiveness indicators: the Competitiveness Index. There are many possible ways of doing this. One would be to include indicators of:

- the business environment: macroeconomic stability, supply side reforms and business perceptions of the UK;

- human and physical capital, technology and research and development;

- innovation: exploitation of science and technology, entrepreneurship, diffusion of knowledge across borders and between firms;

- results: GDP per head, productivity, employment, incomes, and other measures of sustainable development;

Future reports on this Strategy will take account of this work.[4]

6.19 Progressively reducing pressures on the environment and resources is part of the competitiveness challenge. Business needs to create more value with less impact: seizing opportunities to innovate and to enhance competitiveness through better use of physical, human and financial resources, while meeting growing customer demand for more environmentally and socially acceptable goods and services. The term 'eco-efficiency' is sometimes applied to such an approach. The World Business Council for Sustainable Development has identified key elements of eco-efficiency, including reducing the materials intensity of goods and services, enhancing recyclability and durability of goods and reducing dispersion of toxic substances.

6.20 This requires investment in research and development, plant and machinery, and improvements in the skills and capabilities of the work force. The Government will enhance development and take-up of new technologies through a new Sustainable Technologies Initiative, involving Government Departments and Research Councils. It will encourage business improvement through sectoral sustainability strategies which look at economic, environmental and social performance. Through UK and European eco-efficiency initiatives, including the use of the Internet, it will help raise awareness of opportunities, spread best practice and improve networking between sources of advice on eco-efficiency.

Action by business sectors and trade associations

Sectoral sustainability strategies provide the framework for addressing the 'triple bottom line' – integrating action and setting priorities to improve business performance on economic, environmental and social aspects. The Government is encouraging trade associations and other representative bodies to develop and implement strategies within at least six business sectors by the end of 2000, building on existing initiatives and best practice. Sectors responding positively to date include the Aluminium Federation, the British Plastics Federation, the British Printing Industry Federation, the British Retail Consortium, the Chemical Industries Association, the Non Ferrous Alliance, the Soap and Detergent Industry Association, and the Society of Motor Manufacturers and Traders.

---

4   The structure outlined in the box is based on the Index of the Massachusetts Innovation Economy, http://www.mtpc.org/research/indica.htm

Promoting the environmental industry

There are many opportunities for UK business in fast-growing markets for environmental technology, goods and services. The Joint Environmental Markets Unit, run by the Department of Trade and Industry and the Department of the Environment, Transport and the Regions and including Foreign Office staff, helps to promote the UK's environmental industry internationally. It helps UK firms in many sectors, ranging from large markets such as those for water supply and waste water treatment to niche areas such as noise and vibration control.

6.21 There is great scope for improvement. For example, information technology is spawning new sectors of the economy, such as computer software and electronic commerce, of high-value and low environmental impact. Through IT, businesses can improve productivity in ways that have environmental, social and economic advantages – such as video conferencing to reduce the need to travel, or use of E-mail. Increasingly rapid product turnover helps to drive change: in the late 1970s, a third of sales by top US companies were from products introduced in the previous 5 years; by 1995, the proportion was over half.

Key actions and commitments

- New monetary and fiscal framework
- Initiatives to promote competitiveness
- Encourage six sectoral sustainability strategies by the end of 2000

Indicators

Total output of the economy (GDP) (headline)

Investment in public, business and private assets (headline)

Social investment

Rate of inflation

Government borrowing and debt

Competitiveness/productivity (to be developed)

Trade/exports/imports

DEVELOPING SKILLS AND REWARDING WORK

6.22 To meet the challenges of sustainable development, we need a skilled and adaptable labour force and a flexible labour market. To promote jobs and employment, better education and training are essential. In a world which is changing rapidly, people need the skills to adapt, and opportunities to update them throughout their lives.

6.23 At the same time, goods and services should be produced in ways which reward work, and treat employees fairly. We cannot base our economy on low wages and long hours for workers. To do so risks damaging family life and limiting people's ability to become involved in their own communities.

6.24 The Government's policies are based on promoting life long learning, investing in education and skills, making work pay, and helping people from welfare to work – creating a culture of 'work for those who can, security for those who cannot'. In that way, the number of people able to take up employment will increase, allowing the economy to grow without running into skills shortages and wage inflation, which would threaten sustainable development. Helping people into the labour market and improving skills levels is the best way to reduce poverty and social exclusion, and promotes sustainable communities based on employment rather than welfare.

INVESTING IN EDUCATION AND SKILLS

6.25 Standards of education and training have been rising in the UK, but in many respects are still behind European countries and the Pacific Rim. Around a fifth of adults, have poor reading, writing and mathematics skills. In 1997/98, over 6% of 16 year olds left school without any formal qualifications.

6.26 We must raise educational standards at all levels and close the widening gap between high and low achievers. The Government is implementing a new National Literacy and Numeracy strategy in England; and is acting to reduce to 30 and under class sizes for 5-7 year olds. It has set new National Learning Targets for 2002: for example, 85% of 19 year olds to have a 'level 2'[5] qualification.

5   e.g. 5 GCSEs at grade C or above.

6.27 The Family Literacy and Numeracy initiatives will reach parents with poor basic skills and their children. The Government has invested £540 million in the Sure Start programme to improve the emotional and social development, health and readiness to learn of children under four in deprived areas, to help their families and communities.

6.28 The Government's proposals on lifelong learning were set out in its 1998 Green Paper, *The Learning Age*.[6] They aim to develop skills needed for a productive workforce and competitive economy, and to increase participation in learning throughout life, especially among disadvantaged groups.

6.29 The Government's Skills Task Force will advise on skills needs and shortages, as part of the development of a National Skills Agenda. Initiatives to boost workplace and lifelong learning such as Investors in People, Individual Learning accounts, the University for Industry and the Learning Direct telephone helpline will ensure that people can attain and build on educational qualifications and improve their employability. A National Learning Target is for 10,000 small organisations, and 45% of larger bodies,[7] to be recognised as Investors In People by 2002.

Developing skills for a competitive economy

6.30 The 1999 Budget announced a national IT strategy to increase access to and use of IT in communities, homes, businesses and schools, with £470m of funding to create up to 1000 learning centres across the UK.

HELPING PEOPLE FROM WELFARE TO WORK

6.31 Helping people move from welfare to work where they can do so is a Government priority. In Spring 1998, the UK employment rate[8] was around 73%. Around one in six households[9] has at least

Welfare to Work

The New Deal targets groups at risk of exclusion from the labour market, helping them into productive work, improving skills and incomes and increasing the productive workforce for the country as a whole.

By the end of January 1999, over 55,000 young people had moved into sustainable jobs[10] through the **New Deal for Young People**, and over 50,000 had started work experience and training, including through the **Environment Task Force** option. A further 6,800 long-term unemployed people aged 25 and over found jobs thanks to the **New Deal for the long-term unemployed** in the 6 months since its launch.

The New Deal for **lone parents** was launched nationwide in October 1998. Pilot schemes under a New Deal for **disabled people** got underway in September 1998. A New Deal to help the **partners of unemployed people** get back to work began in April 1999, and a New Deal for the **over 50s** was announced in the 1999 Budget.

The **Welfare Reform and Pensions Bill**, now before Parliament, will pave the way for the introduction of Employment Zones and a 'single work-focused gateway' as a single point of access to the benefit system for people of working age, encouraging more people to find work and providing a better service.

6   *The learning age: a renaissance for a new Britain*. February 1998, Cm 3790. ISBN 0 10 137902 1.

7   Small organisations are those with 10-49 employees, larger organisations with 50+.

8   Seasonally adjusted.

9   As at Spring 1997.

10 Defined as where young people had moved into employment and did not claim Jobseeker's Allowance within 3 months.

one person of working age but no-one in employment, and around 210,000 people had been claiming Jobseeker's Allowance for more than two years.[11]

6.32 The Government's approach involves a wide range of initiatives. The programme is funded over this Parliament by the £5.2 billion raised by the windfall tax on excess profits of the privatised utilities. In March 1998, the Welfare Reform Green Paper set out a new contract for welfare aimed at moving working age people not in employment closer to labour markets.[12] The New Deals for unemployed people are a key element, and the Government has also introduced area-based initiatives such as Employment Zones.

FAIR AND REWARDING WORK

6.33 People are reluctant to take work which would leave them little better off than they are on benefits, or to take a better-paying job if they would lose most of the increased income through paying more tax and receiving less benefit. The Government is determined to make work pay. In particular, following the 1999 Budget:

- the Working Families Tax Credit guarantees, from October 1999, a minimum income of £200 per week for working families with a full time earner; other guarantees are provided by the Disabled Person's Tax Credit;

- reforms to National Insurance Contributions will improve work incentives and allow low paid people to take home more of their earnings;

- a 10p starting rate of income tax will halve the tax bills for 1.8 million people, and the basic rate of income tax will be cut to 22p from April 2000, the lowest basic rate of tax for 70 years.

6.34 Promoting social progress includes fairness at work, creating a balance between the rights and responsibilities of workers and employers. A National Minimum Wage took effect on 1 April 1999. The Government has implemented the EU Working Time Directive which, for the first time, gives employees in the UK minimum holiday entitlements and rest periods. The Employment Relations Bill, which follows on from the *Fairness at work* White Paper,[13] takes forward the Government's wider strategy for employment relations, with proposals for individual rights, collective rights and family-friendly policies, including extended maternity leave, parental leave and time-off for family emergencies.

6.35 The Government is investing £470 million in a National Childcare Strategy. This will help parents, especially women, to balance work and family life, helping them to take up employment, education or training. Out of school childcare will become available for every community which needs it. In England, all four year olds are now guaranteed

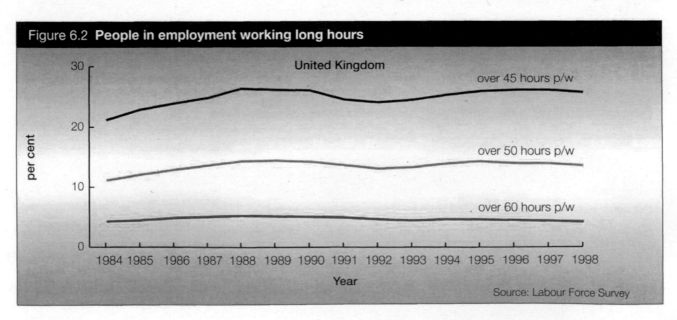

Figure 6.2 **People in employment working long hours**

United Kingdom

over 45 hours p/w

over 50 hours p/w

over 60 hours p/w

per cent

30
20
10
0

1984 1985 1986 1987 1988 1989 1990 1991 1992 1993 1994 1995 1996 1997 1998

Year

Source: Labour Force Survey

11 As at April 1998.

12 *New ambitions for our country: a new contract for welfare.* March 1998, Cm 3805. ISBN 0 10 138052 6.

13 *Fairness at work.* May 1998, Cm 3968. ISBN 0 10 139682 1.

a free at least part-time early education place, and the Government aims to double the proportion of three year olds with free places, to 66% by 2002.

6.36 Businesses need to maintain a safe and healthy environment for their employees, and others who may be affected by their activities. The consequences of not complying with workplace health and safety legislation could be significant for many industrial processes. While standards of workplace health and safety in the UK are high in comparison with many other EU countries, the costs of disability or ill-health arising from accidents in the workplace and work related ill-health have been estimated to cost around 2–3% of GDP. To achieve long term improvement we must provide a regulatory framework that encourages best management practice and a flexible approach. Partnerships between employers, employees and the wider community all contribute to creating work places which enhance health and well-being.

6.37 The Health and Safety Executive plays a key role in ensuring risks to people's health and safety from workplace activities are properly controlled. In the last ten years the fatal injury rate for workers has fallen from 1.8 to 1.0 per hundred thousand and HSE's purpose is to reduce this still further. It aims to achieve this through modernising and simplifying the legal framework, improving compliance with the law, providing better information, and increasing the engagement and participation of others.

PROMOTING FAIRNESS OVERSEAS

6.38 For a trading nation like the UK, the economic and social benefits from trade will continue to be important and can make a significant contribution to sustainable development at home. In addition, the Government is encouraging action to maximise the benefits our trade can bring overseas.

6.39 Consumers are increasingly interested in issues such as fair trade and the use of child labour. A business with extensive interests in developing countries is likely to be involved in social issues, such as education and housing of employees.

Some businesses have made significant efforts to research and improve the social and environmental aspects of their international supply chains.

6.40 The Government is encouraging this process. Its 1997 White Paper on International Development called for world-wide observance of internationally-recognised core labour standards,[14] alongside human rights, environmental standards, and standards of business conduct. It supports the Ethical Trading Initiative, which brings together companies, voluntary organisations and trade unions in efforts to raise the quality of life of workers in global supply chains of companies importing into the UK.

Trade to benefit the poor

The Department for International Development supports trade projects which increase benefits for poor producers and help to integrate the poorest countries into world trade. Measures include assistance with design and quality of products, legal requirements, marketing and certification. The Department has worked with Artisan Trust, Traidcraft and Oxfam, and is also in discussion with more mainstream companies.

6.41 The Government will promote responsible business behaviour by UK companies overseas, including in the poorest countries, through the Department for International Development and Department of Trade and Industry and through the new Global Citizenship Unit in the Foreign Office. Responsible behaviour will take account of environmental, social, and local economic impacts of business, including human rights and corruption. The Government's Green Citizenship Challenge encourages UK companies to give the same priority to the environment overseas as they do at home. Meeting these challenges will enhance the reputation and success of our businesses abroad, as well as benefiting people overseas.

14 As defined in the International Labour Organisation's Declaration on Fundamental Principles and Rights of Work.

Key actions and commitments

- Welfare reform

- Reforming the tax and benefit system

- Minimum wage, Working Time Directive and Employment Relations Bill

- Lifelong learning

- Ethical Trading Initiative

Indicators

Proportion of people of working age who are in work (headline)

Workless households

Long term unemployment

Proportion of lone parents, long term ill and disabled in touch with the labour market

Low pay

People in employment working long hours

Working days lost through illness, work fatalities and injury rates

Qualifications at age 19 (headline)

Adult literacy/numeracy

People without qualifications

Learning participation

Businesses recognised as Investors in People

Ethical trading

Sustainable production and consumption

6.42 To complement the measures mentioned above, we need action focused more directly on the production and use of goods and services. Achieving changes is not a matter of 'picking winners'. Instead, it involves continuous improvements in performance and extension of good practice; designing products so they can be easily upgraded and recycled; new kinds of products and, in some cases, meeting consumer needs through services rather than goods. The Government's approach is to work with the market and encourage entrepreneurship, using a mix of measures to:

- give consumers better information and encouraging purchasing initiatives which help to move the market;

- promote sustainable production by identifying indicators, setting targets and monitoring, promoting best practice, and supporting research and innovation;

- provide a supporting framework of information and investment programmes and, where appropriate, regulatory and fiscal measures.

6.43 This broad approach is often called **'market transformation'**. It seeks to deliver better goods and services to more people, at lower cost and with lower environmental impacts; improving the performance of the best products, while leaving no place for the poorest performers. The Government will build on achievements and encourage similar action in other sectors, recognising that the scope for market transformation, and the mix of measures, will vary from sector to sector.

Market Transformation in action

As part of the European Union's CO_2 from Cars Strategy, a voluntary agreement with the major European motor manufacturers will secure a 25% reduction in carbon dioxide emissions from new cars by 2008. New cars will be subject to mandatory fuel consumption and carbon dioxide emission labelling.

A voluntary, independently monitored, agreement by soap and detergent manufacturers sets production targets and will give consumers better information on detergent use. It seeks to achieve up to 10% reductions in energy use, waste and packaging in the three years to 2001.

6.44 The Government will encourage ways[15] to look at environmental, economic and social impacts at all stages of a product's life cycle – production of raw materials, manufacture, purchase, use and disposal – to help decide on priorities. It will participate in work led by the European Commission on an **Integrated Product Policy**, which aims to modify and improve the environmental performance of product systems, considering the whole life cycle of a product in an integrated way, and addressing everyone in the product chain – industry, retailers and consumers.

ACTION BY CONSUMERS

6.45 The Government will publish a Consumer Strategy White Paper this summer. It will provide a framework within which consumers can make appropriate choices and will focus on helping them to become more knowledgeable and better informed.

6.46 In addition, the Government will give consumers better information on which to act and use purchasing policy to promote change through:

- **Mandatory labelling.** Legal requirements for information apply for some products, such as on energy consumption of household appliances. Similar measures at European level will apply to all new cars from 2000 and are under consideration for domestic boilers and water heaters.

- **Voluntary labelling and product declarations.** Mandatory labelling can cover only a small part of consumer information. Through its **Green Claims Code**, the Government has secured business support for action to deter false or unreliable claims and is inviting proposals for new UK labelling and award initiatives.

- **Purchasing initiatives** can promote more sustainable goods and services and help them become financially viable and competitive. For example, the Energy Saving Trust's Powershift programme for 'alternatively fuelled' vehicles has encouraged major fleet operators to use cars, lorries and buses fuelled by gas and electricity. Purchasing initiatives can help small and medium-sized businesses, who find it difficult to act alone, to make improvements.

- **Government purchasing policy.** The Government is a major procurer and recognises that public purchasers, through pursuing departmental environmental strategies and seeking value for money, will help to influence suppliers, both to offer sustainable goods and services and to become more competitive.

Household appliances like cookers and refrigerators use 25% of UK electricity

15 For example, whole life costing, footprinting, and life cycle analysis.

Pensions

Many people would like their pensions investment to be in companies that are environmentally and socially responsible. The December 1998 Green Paper on Pensions proposed that pension funds trustees should be required to state their policy, if any, on socially responsible, environmentally responsible and ethical investment.[16]

The Government has also set out proposals for a pooled pension investment (ppi), which could provide a flexible and transparent means of investing in pensions. This would enable pension schemes which use the ppi to offer, and scheme members to choose, such methods of investing.

Each department is able to build sustainable development and environmental factors into its contract specifications. Departments are also required to take procurement decisions on the basis of whole life costs, which allows account to be taken of long term savings in areas such as energy efficiency. Purchasers look to work in partnership with suppliers to deliver steady improvements in performance during a contract, for instance through reductions in emissions from transport services.

- **public awareness and promotional programmes**, such as *Are you doing your bit?* and those run by the Energy Saving Trust, reinforce product labelling and purchasing programmes.

Key actions and commitments

- Mandatory and voluntary labelling

- Purchasing initiatives to encourage new goods and services

- Public awareness initiatives, including the new *Are you doing your bit?* campaign

Indicators

Consumer information (to be developed)

Consumer expenditure

SUSTAINABLE PRODUCTION

6.47 Measures to promote more sustainable production will include:

- raising awareness of the potential for increased efficiency. Understanding varies widely across business sectors. Substantial cost saving opportunities remain. The Government's **Best Practice** Programmes for Energy Efficiency, Environmental Technology and Construction are designed to bridge that gap, and have so far helped business make annual savings of £650m in energy costs and £50m in waste costs. The Government is consulting on priorities for extending these Programmes into areas such as freight distribution. A similar programme is under consideration for waste management. The Government will announce shortly a programme of targets for resource and environmental improvements from take-up of best practice in key sectors, based on indicators of energy, water, waste generation, and emissions of hazardous substances.

Awards schemes

Awards schemes can raise the profile of successful companies and public bodies, helping to inform consumers and boost business competitiveness. The Government manages the Queen's Awards, which include an award for Environmental Achievement. The Awards are under review by a committee chaired by the Prince of Wales, which will consider the arguments for broadening the scope of the environment award and ways of addressing sustainable development more widely.

There are over 50 other UK environmental awards. This diversity can blunt the impact of awards, and leads to varying coverage and quality. UK awards promoters are beginning to address this issue through an environmental awards forum, and the Government will support this process.

- **minimum standards** to eliminate processes or products with unacceptable environmental impacts, or to provide a baseline for improvements (such as standards for energy consumption of household appliances and office

16 *A new contract for welfare: partnership in pensions*. December 1998, Cm 4179. ISBN 0 10 141792 6.

equipment). Product standards are under consideration in areas such as lighting components and in the Building Regulations.

- **producer responsibility** initiatives, getting producers to share responsibility for what happens at the end of products' lives. In some cases, such as cars and newspapers, industries have tackled this voluntarily. Where recycling is currently uneconomic, legislation has been needed, partly so that costs are fairly distributed: for example, the Packaging Regulations mean that around half of all packaging will be recycled or recovered by 2001. EU initiatives are under consideration for motor vehicles, batteries, electrical and electronic equipment.

- partnerships along the **supply chain** to help suppliers – often small or medium-sized businesses who find it difficult to act alone – to make improvements. Better environmental performance is often associated with cost saving over the life of a product, benefiting supplier and purchaser alike.

- **commitment by business** to assess impacts and set targets. The Government is working with business sectors to encourage action by individual firms and trade associations. It will also continue to encourage widespread take up of the European environmental management regulation (EMAS) and the International Standards Organisation's system, ISO 14001. It will sponsor work on development of a 'sustainable management system' to help integrate sustainable development into the plans and operations of companies.

Making a Corporate Commitment Campaign

Making a Corporate Commitment (MACC) is a successful energy efficiency campaign which has attracted 2000 members. The Government will relaunch it later this year to embrace other sustainable development issues, helping members to identify their own priorities and approaches for improvements.

- **environmental** reporting by companies to demonstrate business commitment to improvement in environmental performance and to communicate with stakeholders – the workforce, the local community, shareholders and customers. The Government will put in place guidance to allow large businesses to report publicly to a common standard on major environmental impacts. It will look for the top 350 businesses to report to these standards by the end of 2001 and will then work to extend this to the 7000 UK businesses with more than 250 employees. To help this process, it will issue a guide to reporting on greenhouse gas emissions later in 1999, followed by similar guidance on waste and water.

Managing environmental risk

Fund managers, banks and insurers are beginning to take greater account of business environmental performance and management of environmental risk. The UK insurance industry has drawn up guidelines for business on public liability insurance for pollution incidents. Increasingly, businesses that manage environmental risks effectively will pay less than if they expose themselves, their employees, neighbours and insurers to a heavy risk of pollution costs.

Key actions and commitments

- Best Practice Programmes for waste and transport; extension of energy and environment programmes

- develop standards and guidance for environmental reporting and encourage all top UK companies to report publicly on their environmental performance

- relaunch 'Making a Corporate Commitment' campaign

Indicators

Energy and water consumption by sector (to be developed)

Waste and hazardous emissions by sector (to be developed)

Adoption of environmental management systems

Index of corporate environmental engagement

Environmental and sustainable development reporting (to be developed)

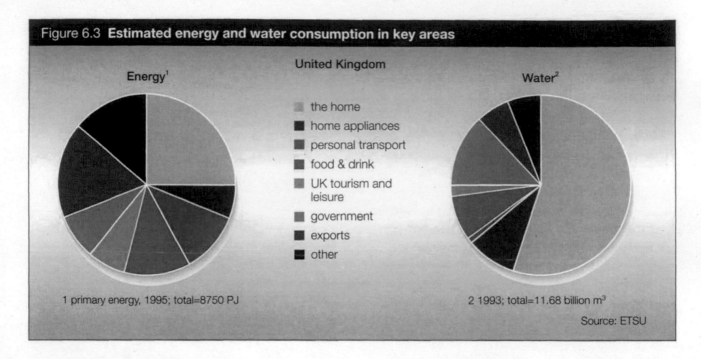

Figure 6.3 Estimated energy and water consumption in key areas

United Kingdom

Energy[1]

Water[2]

- the home
- home appliances
- personal transport
- food & drink
- UK tourism and leisure
- government
- exports
- other

1 primary energy, 1995; total=8750 PJ

2 1993; total=11.68 billion m³

Source: ETSU

KEY AREAS FOR ACTION

6.48 There is scope for change in many areas, but it is essential to identify priorities. One way to do this is to think about 'final consumption': for example, the impacts of agriculture, food manufacture and distribution all relate to the food and drink we consume. Another is to address key sectors of the economy, as in sectoral sustainability strategies. These approaches are complementary. The following paragraphs first look at five major categories of final consumption, taken from Figure 6.3, and then illustrate examples of a sectoral approach.

6.49 Figure 6.3 illustrates estimated resource use and environmental impacts of 'final consumption'; it includes estimates of both direct (for example, fuel for heating) and indirect effects (for example, energy used in extracting raw materials and in making a heating system). The estimates give a broad guide to the environmental impact, but further work is being undertaken to improve them, and to add other impacts, such as amounts of solid waste generated.[17]

THE HOME

6.50 We need housing which better meets people's changing needs and which – in its construction and over its whole life – is more energy efficient, uses fewer resources and creates less waste. That requires action to address both new and existing housing.

6.51 The potential is considerable. Savings from low energy lighting, better insulation, cavity walls, and condensing boilers outweigh costs over a few years. Wider use of simple measures such as low volume flush toilets would quickly reduce water use. Delivering improvements involves:

- **Changing consumer behaviour.** Energy labelling for new housing is now part of the Building Regulations. The Government is considering requiring disclosure of energy ratings for all new homes, and whether an energy efficiency assessment might be included, as part of a survey report, in a seller's pack offered by vendors of existing houses. The Energy Saving Trust promotes energy saving measures, and the Government is considering measures to encourage water and power utilities to help consumers use resources more efficiently.

- **Action by business.** The Energy Saving Trust is helping retailers, manufacturers, installers, energy suppliers and consumer organisations to

17 Direct consumption figures are derived from national statistics on energy use and expenditure on water; indirect consumption has been estimated from Office for National Statistics Input – Output tables showing the flow of products between business sectors. (Source ETSU 1999).

work together to deliver energy efficient goods and services. Resource efficiency is a priority for the industry-led Movement for Innovation and Housing Forum and the Construction Best Practice Programme.

- **Government action.** The first phase of a review of energy efficiency and the Building Regulations took place in 1998. Investment in housing can improve housing quality and efficiency: around 2 million homes will benefit from the extra £5 billion which the Government is making available for this purpose over the life of this Parliament.

6.52 Over the next 10-25 years, there is further scope for benefits through changes such as:

- **'Intelligent' buildings,** with improved control systems integrating different services systems and taking account of occupant behaviour patterns and external climate changes.

- **Energy efficient homes** with more dynamic insulation, heat recovery systems and excellent air tightness. Incorporation of photovoltaics, active solar panels, ground source heat pumps, and Combined Heat and Power for grouped housing.

- **Greater use of sustainable construction materials and prefabrication.** Timber from sustainable sources, recycled alternatives such as plastic from other industries and recycled construction waste, and composite materials which recycle low grade substances such as agricultural waste fibre or low quality plastics would all reduce the burden on primary aggregates.

6.53 The Government will work with industry to promote such changes: for example, by working with the construction industry on a strategy for more sustainable construction (see box on sectoral examples after 6.72).

6.54 The Department of the Environment, Transport and the Regions is taking forward a number of its Property Advisory Group's suggestions for securing more environmentally sustainable buildings in the commercial sector, including offices, shops, restaurants, warehouses and factories.

Key actions and commitments

- Energy labelling for housing

- Industry initiatives for resource efficiency

- Sustainable construction and review of Building Regulations

Indicators

Household water use and peak demand

Thermal efficiency of housing stock

Primary aggregates per unit of construction value

Construction waste going to landfill

Home appliances

6.55 Home appliances make domestic tasks easier and allow better access to commercial, leisure and educational opportunities. For the future, we need more efficient appliances, and changes in the way we use them. Appliances such as lights, cookers, refrigerators, washing machines, computers, televisions and videos consume around 25% of UK electricity. It is a fast growing sector – overall energy use by appliances, other than lighting, has almost doubled since 1990; around 50% of households are expected to be connected to the Internet by 2010.

6.56 Market transformation is well under way. There are already major differences in products. The most efficient washing machine on sale in the UK uses a quarter of the energy of the least efficient and half of the average machine. A similar story applies to other appliances.

6.57 Action for change is based on the type of measures outlined in paragraphs 6.46 and 6.47. The Government has published specific strategies on lighting, washing machines, dishwashers and tumble dryers. Other sectors covered include heating, cooking, refrigeration, televisions and videos, office equipment and motors.

Key actions and commitments

- Stimulate market transformation of domestic appliances

Indicators

Energy efficiency of new appliances

FOOD AND DRINK

Food safety and standards

6.58 Achieving sustainable development means producing affordable and good quality food and drink in accordance with high environmental and animal welfare standards. The Government has published draft legislation to establish the Food Standards Agency. The main objective of this new body will be the protection of public health in relation to food. The Agency, which will have powers to take action across the whole food chain, will be an open and authoritative body able to speak up for consumers. Consumers in the UK are also increasingly demanding assurances about the welfare standards of farm animals. The Government's aim is to maintain, and where possible improve, the high standards already found in this country.

6.59 One aspect of food safety of particular concern is pesticides. These are subject to strict regulatory control to ensure that any residues in food are at acceptable levels. All pesticides are subject to rigorous scientific evaluation before approval for use is given. The approvals system is backed up by a wide-ranging surveillance programme designed to check that both domestically produced and imported food complies with statutory maximum residue levels. The results of this programme are published in full in the annual reports of the Working Party on Pesticide Residues.

Farming and the countryside

6.60 Agriculture has a vital role to play in protecting and enhancing our countryside, and contributing to the rural economy and rural communities. Overall agricultural policy is determined by the EU Common Agricultural Policy (CAP). While this has been very successful in securing reliable food supplies, public expectations from a common agricultural policy have changed with increased concern about the impact of agricultural activity upon the environment.

6.61 The Government strongly supports reform of the CAP, away from the support for production and towards support for rural development and the environment. The agreement on Agenda 2000/CAP reform at the Special European Council in Berlin in March 1999 represents real progress, with cuts in price support (compensated as direct payments), and the creation of an integrated rural development policy, including agri-environmental measures, which will provide in principle the basis for a shift of emphasis from production support

Consumers are concerned that food should be produced to high standards

towards environmental and rural development measures in the future.

6.62 To help farmers in their dual roles as food producers and stewards of the countryside, the Government operates a wide-ranging package of voluntary incentive schemes and advice on best practice. Following the 1998 Comprehensive Spending Review, the Government is making £40 million available over the next three years to expand these schemes. This includes extra funding of £20 million for the scheme to help farmers to convert to organic production methods. Revised Codes of Good Agricultural Practice for the Prevention of Pollution of Water, Air and Soil have been published, and details have been sent to all farmers.

6.63 Advice is also provided to encourage the best use of pesticides in a number of ways. The Government's policy is that the amount of pesticide should be the minimum necessary to ensure effective pest control. A key objective is to minimise the impact of pesticides on human health and the environment. The Pesticides Forum, which brings together environmental and agricultural interests, has developed an action plan to promote the responsible use of pesticides. In addition, the Government is funding a wide-ranging research and development programme investigating, among other issues, non-chemical means of pest and disease control. The Government has also commissioned research on the possible impact and design of a tax or charge on pesticides and will seek views on the issues raised before reaching a conclusion.

6.64 A contentious area at present is the development of genetically modified crops. At the farm level, the Government's approach is based on full ecological evaluation of field-scale plantings before commercial crops are planted. This approach means that we shall be able to identify any problems in time to take appropriate action, at the same time as being able to assess the potential benefits for the environment and for farmers alike.

6.65 The Government is also developing a pilot set of indicators of sustainable agriculture. These are intended to provide a means of measuring the economic, social and environmental impacts of agriculture and help assess the effectiveness of policies and sustainability of the sector. These indicators will complement the main set of indicators mentioned in chapter 3 and will also be published later in 1999.

6.66 Most of the UK's land area is in agricultural use. How that land is used is clearly vital to sustainable development, including taking the right decisions about protecting it from inappropriate development. Agricultural land is an important natural resource and great care is needed over decisions about its use in order to safeguard the needs of future generations.

Key actions and commitments

- Establish Foods Standards Agency
- Reform of Common Agricultural Policy

Indicators

Pesticide residues in food

Area under agreement under the Environmentally Sensitive Area and Countryside Stewardship agri-environment schemes

Area converted to organic production

PERSONAL TRANSPORT

6.67 Energy-efficient and resource-efficient vehicles are needed for sustainable transport, alongside measures to influence transport use (see chapter 7). The next few years will see alternative fuels; better engine technology; and redesign to reduce vehicle weight.

6.68 The Government supports the EU's strategy to reduce average carbon dioxide emissions from new cars by up to 40% by 2010 at the latest. As part of this strategy, the European Commission has already secured a voluntary agreement with European car manufacturers to reduce such emissions by about 25% by 2008. All new cars must be labelled to show fuel consumption and carbon dioxide emissions.

6.69 The Government is also using fiscal measures, such as the fuel duty escalator, graduated Vehicle

Excise Duty, and reform of company car taxation to encourage more fuel efficient vehicles. Initiatives such as Powershift, the Foresight Vehicle Programme and the Cleaner Vehicles Task Force are encouraging research and promotion of cleaner vehicles.

CLEANER VEHICLES TASK FORCE

The Cleaner Vehicles Task Force aims to encourage production, marketing, purchase and use of vehicles that are more fuel efficient, less polluting, quieter and less resource intensive, and to improve the environmental performance of existing vehicles. It is a partnership between Government, industry, non-Governmental organisations and other stakeholders. Its first report, published in May 1999, contains a number of key recommendations including the establishment of a voluntary green fleet certification scheme.

Key actions and commitments

- Mandatory labelling of motor vehicles

- First Report of Cleaner Vehicles Task Force

Indicators

Energy efficiency of road passenger travel

Average fuel consumption of new cars

TOURISM AND LEISURE

6.70 Tourism is a major industry in Britain. In February 1999, the Government published *Tomorrow's Tourism*, a new strategy for tourism in England[18]. Strategies have also been published in Scotland and Northern Ireland, and one is being prepared for Wales.

6.71 The Government wishes to see the UK tourism industry grow significantly, in ways which are economically, socially and environmentally beneficial. The approach set out in *Tomorrow's Tourism* includes:

- **establishing an effective policy framework:** a new strategic body will lead in developing sustainable tourism. The forthcoming Urban and Rural White Papers (see chapter 7) will take account of tourism's contribution to quality of life;

- **maximising tourism's potential to benefit communities,** by encouraging local goods, services and employment, and tourism's role in improving local environments;

- **managing visitor flows,** through more effective visitor management plans;

- **addressing transport and planning issues:** integrating tourism with public transport, and ensuring that tourism development respects the local built and natural environment;

- **building partnerships** between public, private and voluntary sectors: for example, the Building Research Establishment is planning a new programme to reduce energy consumption by tourism businesses.

6.72 Increased access to tourism for all is a priority. *Tomorrow's Tourism* sets out measures to help people who find difficulty in taking holidays: elderly people, people with disabilities, single parent families, families with young children, carers and people with low incomes.

Key actions and commitments

- Implement Tourism Strategy

Indicators

Pressure on key sites (to be developed)

Overseas travel

Leisure trips by mode of transport

---

18 *Tomorrow's Tourism – a growth industry for the new Millennium.* Department for Culture, Media and Sport, February 1999.

Sectoral examples

- The construction industry, including repair, maintenance and improvement of buildings, accounts for some 10% of GDP in the UK and employs 1.5 million people. Buildings consume energy and materials, not only in their construction, but in their lifetime operation as well, generating waste and pollution. The Government is working with the industry and its major clients to take forward the recommendations of Sir John Egan's Task Force which will enable the industry to work towards improving its performance and sustainability. The Government and industry are also developing a strategy, to be launched in the autumn, for achieving more sustainable construction. This will include agreed sectoral targets covering areas such as waste minimisation and use of recycled materials, and whole life costing. The Construction Best Practice Programme will help promote the messages of this strategy to the industry.

- The chemical industry provides many modern consumer goods. Some companies have re-appraised services and products to reduce environmental impact and increase profits. But gaps remain in understanding of environmental impacts. A consultation in 1998 will be followed by a chemicals strategy, including measures for quicker decisions on assessing and managing risks.

- Distribution is the link between production and sale. In March 1999, the Government published *Sustainable Distribution: A Strategy*, to help industry develop distribution systems which support economic growth, protect the environment and benefit society. It seeks to reduce waste through better use of assets, lower energy consumption, minimising vehicle operations and best use of existing infrastructure, including rail, waterways and coastal shipping. Measures include fiscal instruments; strategic planning to integrate transport networks; better regulation to improve safety and ensure fair competition; and partnerships with industry to promote best practice.

- Air traffic is expected to double by 2015. The Government is preparing a UK airports policy looking some 30 years ahead. To maximise the contribution they make to local and regional economies and to reduce pressure in south east England, the Government will encourage growth of regional airports to meet local demand for air travel, where consistent with sustainable development objectives. The Government believes that aviation should meet its external costs, including environmental costs, and will work with other countries to develop tighter standards on noise and emissions, and to examine the potential for economic instruments to encourage the use of quieter, less polluting aircraft.

Key actions and commitments

- Strategy for Sustainable Construction
- Publish Chemical Strategy before end 1999
- Implement Sustainable Distribution Strategy

Indicators

Chemical releases to the environment (to be developed)

Freight transport by mode

Heavy goods vehicle mileage intensity

CHAPTER 7

Building Sustainable Communities

We need to build sustainable communities in our cities, towns and rural areas by:

- strengthening regional and local economies;

- meeting people's social needs: promoting better health, housing and access to services and recreation;

- improving local surroundings: revitalising town centres, tackling degraded urban environments, and ensuring that development respects the character of our countryside;

- reducing crime and the fear of crime;

- addressing problems of poverty and social exclusion in the most deprived communities;

- making it easier for people to get involved in their communities;

- co-ordinating policies to bring these objectives together.

7.1   Thriving regions, cities, towns, villages and neighbourhoods are fundamental to quality of life. Strong economies, employment opportunities, good access to services, and attractive and safe surroundings are vital for their sustainable development. We need to achieve these in ways which make good use of natural resources, protect the environment and promote social cohesion.

7.2   Wherever we look, there are connections. Improving health involves tackling poverty, poor housing and degraded local environments. Policies on urban living and rural development go hand in hand with those to protect the countryside. Locating development and services to reduce the need for travel is essential if we are to tackle road traffic growth and climate change.

7.3   We need policies which make these links. The Government is delivering these in areas such as regional development, planning, transport, health, housing, regeneration, and local government. An integrated approach is also needed at other levels, for example in regional organisations and local government.

7.4   The skills and enthusiasm of local people, voluntary bodies, and business are vital for change. Building sustainable communities is about improvements to the places where people live and work, and giving them the chance to play their part in shaping change.

Promoting economic vitality and employment

7.5   To build sustainable communities right across the country, prosperity and employment opportunities need to be widely distributed. There are considerable regional disparities in economic performance. We need to increase prosperity at regional and local level while maintaining and enhancing other aspects of quality of life. National initiatives to promote skills, investment and job opportunities, outlined in chapter 6, must be complemented by action at regional and local level.

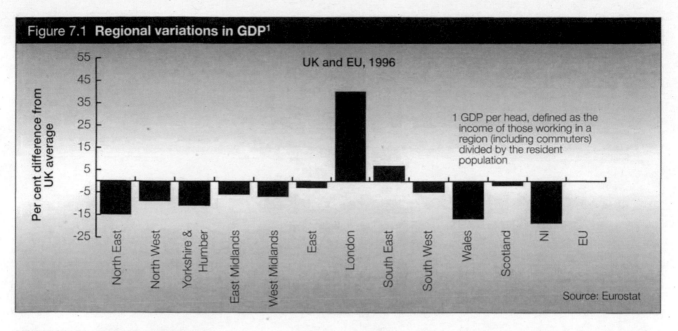

Figure 7.1 **Regional variations in GDP**[1]

UK and EU, 1996

Per cent difference from UK average

1 GDP per head, defined as the income of those working in a region (including commuters) divided by the resident population

North East, North West, Yorkshire & Humber, East Midlands, West Midlands, East, London, South East, South West, Wales, Scotland, NI, EU

Source: Eurostat

REGIONAL DEVELOPMENT

7.6   In England, Regional Development Agencies (RDAs) will develop and implement strategies which relate to their statutory purposes: economic development and regeneration; business efficiency and skills; innovation and competitiveness; employment, and sustainable development. The strategies will aim to improve economic performance, enhance regional competitiveness and provide regional frameworks which will ensure a better strategic focus for and co-ordination of activity in the region, whether at regional or local level.

7.7   RDAs have been given guidance which stresses the need for them to take an integrated and sustainable approach to regional economic issues, tackling business competitiveness and the need to increase productivity, and the underlying problems of unemployment, skills shortages and physical decay. RDAs will join up and develop links between these areas. Their strategies will set the framework for economic decision-taking in their regions, whether by Government, the RDAs, or other bodies at regional and local levels.

7.8   In Wales, the Welsh Development Agency exists to further economic development, to promote industrial efficiency and international competitiveness, and to improve the environment. Sustainable development, including the creation of sustainable communities, is at the heart of its aims.

7.9   *Pathway to Prosperity: a new economic agenda for Wales* was published by the Welsh Office in July 1998. Its objectives are to spread prosperity throughout Wales, to raise employment rates, and to reduce the gap in GDP per head between Wales and the rest of the UK.

7.10   In Northern Ireland, each of the five agencies currently working for the economic development of the region has a remit to take account of the Government's overall policy on sustainable development.

LOCAL PROSPERITY

7.11   Local communities need to share in growing overall prosperity. In general, sustainable local economies will include a robust mix of businesses and job opportunities. Areas heavily dependent on a single industry or employer can be least able to adapt to change. A climate which favours formation of new small businesses helps to promote local business diversity. In its Competitiveness White Paper and in the 1999 Budget, the Government outlined measures to achieve this.

7.12   Encouraging local enterprise and local products does not imply that local communities should be 'self-sufficient', meeting all their needs from within their own boundaries. While it is important not to overlook the environmental impacts of transport, an exclusive focus on local products is neither feasible nor necessary. It would ignore the interdependence of areas, regions and countries; and the aspirations of people in the UK and in developing countries to improve their standards of living through trade.

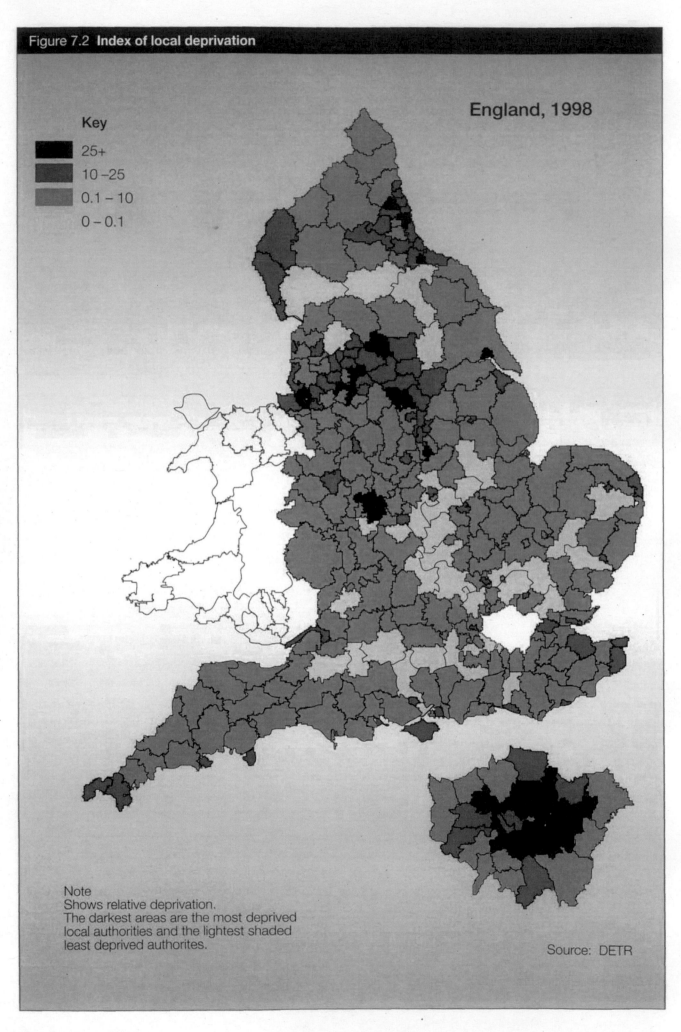

Figure 7.2 **Index of local deprivation**

England, 1998

Key

- 25+
- 10 –25
- 0.1 – 10
- 0 – 0.1

Note
Shows relative deprivation.
The darkest areas are the most deprived
local authorities and the lightest shaded
least deprived authorites.

Source: DETR

EXTENDING OPPORTUNITY

7.13 Over the last twenty years, the number of people in relative poverty has risen sharply, particularly in the 1980s, and the numbers in workless households have doubled. The UK has seen a rise in income inequality almost unique among developed countries. Closing the gap between the poorest communities and the rest is a particular challenge. Around 65 local authority areas in England have high levels of deprivation, many more contain pockets of severe deprivation.

7.14 The seeds of poverty and lack of opportunity are sown in childhood. Children who grow up in disadvantaged families are less likely to succeed in education, and more likely to be disadvantaged as adults. Yet households with children are disproportionately likely to be poor. In March 1999, the Prime Minister set out the Government's aim of ending child poverty over the next twenty years.

7.15 Work and access to work are the key to tackling poverty and extending opportunity. The policies set out in chapter 6, including the £5.2 billion of welfare to work initiatives, are designed to address this. And we have to deal with inter-related problems of unemployment, crime, poor health, housing, and education, and degraded local surroundings. In 1997, the Government set up the Social Exclusion Unit to co-ordinate and improve policies to tackle such problems in England. Its recent work on poor neighbourhoods has led to the establishment of 18 Policy Action Teams. Their work will lead, in the next year, to a national strategy for neighbourhood renewal. Action is also under way in Scotland, Wales and Northern Ireland.

7.16 Action targeted at specific communities and groups is important, building on national initiatives such as on welfare to work. For example:

- the Government is setting up Employment Zones, which will try out new approaches to help people in areas with high long-term unemployment to obtain and keep jobs;

- Education Action Zones have been set up to raise standards in clusters of schools facing challenging circumstances;

- the recently announced 'Excellence in Cities' programme will raise standards of education, create new opportunities and tackle barriers to learning in inner cities;

- the New Deal for Communities is a regeneration programme in England which will tackle problems of multiple deprivation;

- a Policy Action Team established by the Social Exclusion Unit will produce an action plan with targets for reducing disproportionate unemployment among ethnic minorities. Young black men are two to three times as likely to be unemployed as white men with similar educational qualifications;

- in rural areas, the former Rural Development Commission's work on social exclusion is being continued by the new Countryside Agency;

- the Government is investing an additional £354 million in regeneration of coalfield areas, in response to the Coalfields Task Force Report.

New Deal for Communities

The New Deal for Communities is a major new programme to fund regeneration of some of the poorest neighbourhoods, addressing problems such as poor job prospects, high levels of crime, educational underachievement and poor health. It will promote innovative local solutions, supporting partnerships of local people, community and voluntary organisations, public agencies, local authorities and business. The Government will ensure that it is integrated with initiatives such as those on employment and education.

The Government has asked partnerships to take account of sustainable development, and to seek opportunities for using previously developed and vacant urban sites and locating facilities which are readily accessible by public transport, cycling or walking.

7.17 The Government will report annually on overall progress to tackle the causes of poverty and social exclusion. The first report will be published later in 1999. It will include a range of indicators covering such areas as unemployment, low educational attainment, poor housing, and poor health, which can be used in assessing success in reducing poverty and social exclusion.

7.18 There are often opportunities for local projects to promote regeneration and employment to reinforce other sustainable development objectives. Guidance on bids for funding under the Government's Single Regeneration Budget explains that they should take sustainable development into account, and the Department of the Environment, Transport and the Regions has published a best practice guide on sustainable regeneration.

Key actions and commitments

- Regional Development Agencies in England formulating strategies for their regions which contribute to sustainable development

- Sustainable development at the heart of economic development bodies in Wales and Northern Ireland

- Social Exclusion Unit to produce a national strategy for neighbourhood renewal in England

- New Deal for Communities

- Annual report on Government's strategy to reduce poverty and social exclusion

Indicators

Index of Local Deprivation

Regional variations in GDP

Indicators of success in tackling poverty and social exclusion (to be developed)

New business start ups and failures

Ethnic minority unemployment

Indicators of employment in chapter 6

Regeneration for sustainable development

In the South Wales Valleys, the Taff Bargoed Community Revival Strategy has used Welsh Office, Welsh Development Agency, European and Millennium grants to refurbish the former British Coal Trelewis drift mine for business development, training and associated uses, and for environmental works. Over 200 jobs are expected. A Community Park is being created on derelict land and the Welsh International Climbing Centre forms the centrepiece of an outdoor environmental and leisure complex.

Meeting social needs

BETTER HEALTH FOR ALL

7.19 Health has improved enormously this century. In 1900, 154 babies in every thousand in England and Wales died before the age of one, compared with 6 now. Male life expectancy in England and Wales was around 45 years. Now it is around 74 years.

7.20 But more can be done. Life expectancy in Britain is less than in several other European countries. Health inequalities have grown since the early 1980s. Environmental factors still affect health: up to 24,000 vulnerable people are estimated to die prematurely each year because of exposure to air pollution, much of which is due to road traffic.

7.21 The National Health Service will continue to provide people with access to effective health care, based on patients' needs, and not on where they live or their ability to pay. As the proportion of older people in the population increases, the Government is aiming to raise the quality of services for this group.

7.22 Improved health is not just about a better National Health Service. We need to think about the causes of ill health and how to secure healthier life spans, not simply longer ones. We have to address pollution, unhealthy lifestyles, poverty,

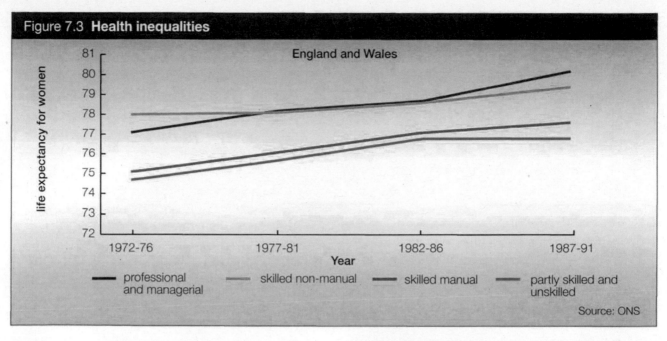

Figure 7.3 **Health inequalities**

England and Wales

life expectancy for women — vertical axis (72–81)

Year — horizontal axis: 1972-76, 1977-81, 1982-86, 1987-91

Legend: professional and managerial · skilled non-manual · skilled manual · partly skilled and unskilled

Source: ONS

worklessness, poor housing, and low educational attainment, all of which the Acheson Report[1] on health inequalities confirmed as major factors leading to poor health.

7.23 The Government's 1998 Green Paper, *Our Healthier Nation*[2], outlined a strategy to deliver key health targets in England based on:

- healthy schools: improving health awareness of young people, and health promotion in schools. The Department of Health and the Department for Education and Employment launched the Healthy Schools Initiative in May 1998;

- healthy workplaces: promoting health (including health and safety) in business and organisational life through the Healthy Workplace Initiative, with the message *Improving Health is Everyone's Business*. This joint initiative with the Health And Safety Commission/Executive involves employers, workers, trades unions and health professionals working together to create healthier workplaces.

- healthy neighbourhoods: reinforcing cross-sector action at local level. Health Action Zones are being set up to reduce health inequalities and improve services, through partnerships between the NHS, local authorities, community groups, the voluntary sector and business.

Our Healthier Nation

The Green Paper, *Our Healthier Nation*, proposed a national target in each of four priority areas:

- to reduce by 2010 the death rate from heart disease, stroke and related illnesses amongst people under 65 by at least a third;

- to reduce by 2010 the death rate from cancer amongst people under 65 by at least a fifth;

- to reduce by 2010 the death rate from suicide and undetermined injury by at least a sixth;

- to reduce by 2010 the rate of accidents by at least a fifth.

7.24 The Government will publish its Health White Paper shortly; a separate Scottish White Paper was published in February 1999[3]. In Wales, the Welsh Office issued a consultation paper *Better Health, Better Wales*[4], in 1998. The Government has published *Well into 2000*, which sets out its vision for improving health and well-being in Northern Ireland. In addition, the Government is reviewing the UK National Environmental Health Action Plan for the World Health Organisation's Ministerial conference on environment and health in London in June 1999.

1 Acheson Report: Independent Enquiry into Inequalities in Health Report, 1998. ISBN 0 11 322173 8
2 *Our Healther Nation: a contract for health*. February 1998, Cm 3854. ISBN 0 10 138522 6.
3 *Towards a healthier Scotland: a White Paper on health*. February 1999, Cm 4269. ISBN 0 10 142692 5.
4 *Better Health, Better Wales*. May 1998, Cm 3922. ISBN 0 10 139222 2.

Health and sustainable development

- The World Health Organisation's Healthy Cities Programme promotes an integrated approach to enhance people's physical, social, mental and environmental well-being. Glasgow, Liverpool, Belfast, and Camden & Islington are long-standing participants, and Newcastle, Stoke-on-Trent, Sheffield, and Manchester have recently been designated within an expanded programme in the European Region. London also hopes to become a World Healthy City under the global WHO programme currently in development.

- 'Improvements in health' is a key theme of Lancashire County Council's Green Audit. Indicators of low birth weight, death rates, years of life lost and long term illness are part of a broad picture of sustainable development which considers links between health and factors such as unemployment.

7.25 At local level, sustainable development and health strategies must reinforce each other. Health features in many Local Agenda 21 strategies (see 7.80). Locally run Healthy Living Centres, funded through the National Lottery New Opportunities Fund, will reach about 20% of the population and will address wider issues affecting health, including access to services. Small-scale, local initiatives can promote health and well-being through improvements in diet, exercise and self-esteem.

Food for health

- Gardening for Health is a community gardening project set up within Bradford's Bangladeshi community to encourage community participation, physical activity, healthy eating and relaxation, and to provide social support for Bangladeshi women who may be particularly isolated from wider society.

- Clayton Brook Food Co-operative was set up in 1996 by residents on a Housing Association owned estate in Lancashire. The estate had few facilities and no local access to fresh fruit and vegetables. The volunteer run co-op has grown to more than 130 members. It has provided access to fresh food, boosted the image of the estate and inspired a further community initiative. *Source: LGMB.*

LESS TRAVEL, BETTER ACCESS

7.26 The car has brought many economic and social benefits. But journeys are getting longer, and more are made by car. The cost of congestion runs into billions of pounds each year. Road transport is a major source of carbon dioxide emissions. Air pollution from traffic damages health.

7.27 The dominance of the car limits choice and opportunity, constraining the transport options available, particularly for those without a car. Inadequate public transport and services which are difficult to reach add to hardship for the least well-off. In England, 75% of rural parishes have a limited bus service, 70% no general store, and over 80% no general practitioner based in the parish.

7.28 We need good public transport, well maintained roads and better conditions for cyclists and pedestrians. We need to consider our own lifestyles – not driving where walking is a straightforward alternative. And we need better access to services with less need to travel. The link between rising prosperity and increased travel must be broken.

7.29 In its 1998 White Papers in England[5] and Scotland,[6] and supporting documents in Wales[7] and Northern Ireland,[8] the Government set out a radical new integrated transport policy, designed to:

- improve choice in transport;

- reduce the need to travel while improving access to education, jobs, leisure and services;

- reduce environmental impacts from transport: on greenhouse gas emissions, air pollution and noise, habitats and wildlife;

- improve transport safety and security.

5   *A New Deal for Transport: Better for Everyone*. The Government's White Paper on the future of Transport, July 1998, CM3950, ISBN 0 10 139502 7.

6   *Travel choices for Scotland:* the Scottish integrated transport White Paper. Scottish Office, July 1998. ISBN 0 10 140102 7.

7   *Transport in Wales into the Future:* Welsh Transport Policy Statement. Transport Policy Division, Welsh Office.

8   *Moving Forward:* Northern Ireland Transport Policy Statement. Department of the Environment for Northern Ireland, November 1998.

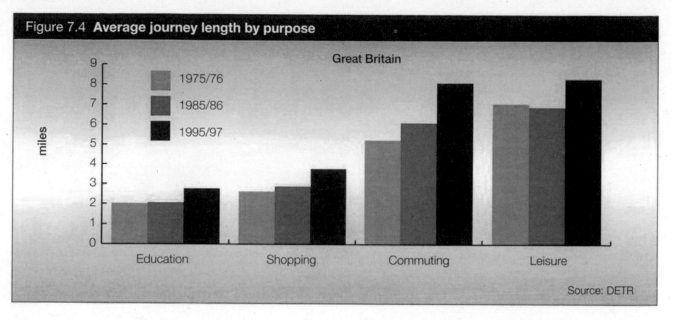

Figure 7.4 **Average journey length by purpose**

Great Britain

miles

Legend: 1975/76, 1985/86, 1995/97

Education · Shopping · Commuting · Leisure

Source: DETR

7.30 Policy measures include:

- local transport plans;

- revisions to planning guidance and new regional transport strategies in England with emphasis on siting major developments where good public transport exists or can be ensured;

- powers for local authorities to levy charges on road users or on workplace parking, with revenues ploughed back into better local transport;

- a new Strategic Rail Authority; and measures to ensure better bus services and better management and maintenance of trunk roads and motorways;

- promoting alternatives to the car through green transport and school travel plans.

7.31 A new Commission for Integrated Transport will advise on targets, including for public transport and on road traffic.

7.32 Everyone has a part to play. The Government is working to help business and other organisations, such as schools and hospitals, to develop Green Transport Plans to reduce the impacts of travel to and during work. Government Departments have targets for introducing such plans by March 1999 in larger buildings, and March 2000 elsewhere. The Government is also promoting safer travel to school through the School Travel Advisory Group and by working in partnership with groups like Sustrans and the Pedestrians Association.

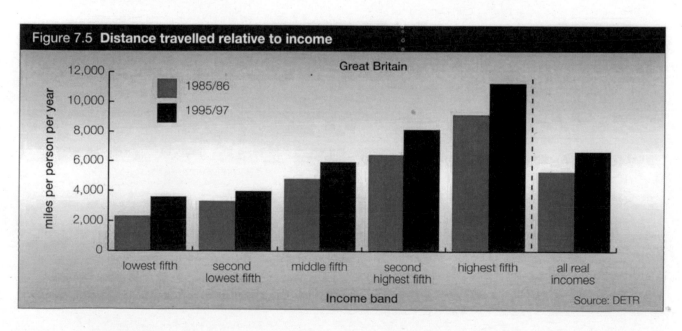

Figure 7.5 **Distance travelled relative to income**

Great Britain

miles per person per year

Legend: 1985/86, 1995/97

lowest fifth · second lowest fifth · middle fifth · second highest fifth · highest fifth · all real incomes

Income band

Source: DETR

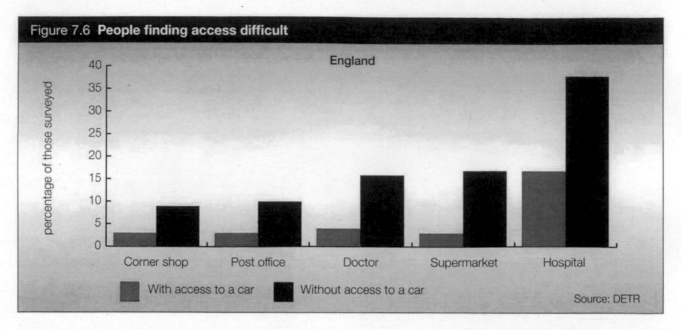

Figure 7.6 **People finding access difficult**

England

percentage of those surveyed

■ With access to a car   ■ Without access to a car

Source: DETR

7.33 Basic services – a supermarket, post office, doctor, clinic, chemist or launderette – are often either non-existent in poor neighbourhoods, or charge high prices. Crime and poor public transport have added to these problems. One of the Policy Action Teams established by the Social Exclusion Unit is developing a strategy to improve access to shopping in deprived areas.

7.34 Access is a key issue for disabled people. The Disability Discrimination Act will ensure that disabled people have access to a wider range of goods, services and facilities. The measures will benefit others, including parents with children in prams and the elderly.

7.35 Access to services is not easy to measure. A sustainable development indicator needs to reflect ease of access by means other than a car. Nor does distance from services tell the whole story. In future, the potential for using information technology to improve access to services will grow. We should develop that potential in ways which do not add to social exclusion or lead to further dispersal of settlement.

COMMUNITY ENTERPRISE AND FINANCIAL SERVICES

7.36 Community-based enterprises can provide access to goods or services in areas where they might not otherwise be available or affordable, or enhance existing services. They often support other objectives – developing skills, creating and retaining wealth within communities, and improving local environments. In some cases, social objectives take precedence over commercial financial returns.

7.37 The Government will continue to encourage innovative community enterprise, in particular through the Single Regeneration Budget (SRB). Under Round 5 of the SRB, local partnerships can devote up to 10% of their funding to projects such as credit unions, development trusts, local exchange and trading systems (LETS) and community enterprise.

Community Enterprise schemes

Liverpool Furniture Resource Centre was formed nine years ago as a traditional furniture recycling scheme. It evolved to refurbish then manufacture furniture for rented accommodation, giving tenants access to accommodation with higher quality furniture than they could otherwise afford. Housing providers benefit through the incentive it gives for take up of empty properties, and those involved in production and distribution have benefited from training.

Source: Enabling Community Enterprise, LGMB 1998

7.38 Most of us take access to affordable loans for granted. But in deprived areas traditional forms of borrowing – for example from mainstream banks – are not always available. Local credit unions – self-help organisations for savings and low cost loans, which are owned and managed by their members – can address problems of personal debt and can, to some extent, provide loan finance to members setting themselves up in business. Credit unions need to be financially viable if they are to have a future and one of the Policy Action Teams set up by the Social Exclusion Unit is currently considering how they might be most effectively funded and operated.

St Malachy's Credit Union

This not for profit company, set up in 1989, offers financial services to people living or working in the area around St Malachy's Roman Catholic Church in Illingworth, Halifax. It encourages members to save regularly, however small the amount. It also aims to provide members with access to low cost credit and a junior section in local schools allows children to improve their money management skills.

Source: Forum for the Future Local Economy Programme

ACCESS TO CULTURE AND SPORT

7.39 The arts and sport make a significant contribution to quality of life and should be accessible to everyone. They can also contribute significantly to regeneration and bring communities together.

7.40 The Government has an overall aim of 'Sport for All'. To ensure increased access in England, Sport England (formerly the English Sports Council), through the Lottery Sports Fund, will be aiming to fund the creation of 6,000 new sports facilities and to establish a new fund for projects which will enhance sporting opportunities for over 2 million people.

7.41 As part of work towards a national strategy for neighbourhood renewal, a Policy Action Team is looking at how to maximise the benefit of arts, sport and leisure for poor neighbourhoods, and particularly disaffected young people and ethnic minorities. The National Lottery distributors are

also being encouraged to demonstrate how their strategies contribute to better access and neighbourhood regeneration.

Sport makes a significant contribution to quality of life

7.42 The New Audiences Fund aims to increase access to the arts throughout England. Grants are made to pilot projects which tackle audience development issues and access in rural areas. These can be specialised marketing initiatives or as simple as tying in free transport from outlying rural areas with specific performances.

ACCESS TO HOUSING

7.43 Decent, energy efficient homes contribute to social cohesion, improved health and better use of fossil fuels and other resources. Housing plays a key role in urban renewal and local regeneration.

7.44 The Government aims to offer everyone the opportunity of a decent home. Most people in the UK want to own their homes: 68% of households in England are now owner-occupiers, compared with only 10% in 1900. The Government supports home ownership mainly through its economic policies, promoting stability in the housing market and ensuring a fair deal for consumers. For those who need help with housing, the Government provides cash benefits to cover individuals' housing costs, subsidies for housing let at sub-market rents by local councils and social landlords, and grants to organisations who help vulnerable members of society. Financial support is backed up by statutory obligations to help people in priority need, such as homeless households.

7.45 Most UK housing is of good quality and the overall condition of the stock is improving. However, just over 7% of the stock in England fails the current fitness standard. In England, a quarter of people from ethnic minorities, a quarter of unemployed people, and nearly one in five lone parents are in poor housing.

7.46 In addition, while overall demand for housing grows, there is a decline in demand in some areas, with near abandonment of neighbourhoods in a few cases. In England just under 4% of the housing stock is vacant.[9] The vast majority of those properties are privately owned. There is scope to make better use of empty homes, although a certain level of vacancies is necessary for an efficient housing market and to allow mobility.

7.47 The Government is making available an extra £5 billion for investment in housing during this Parliament. This will enable local authorities to tackle housing in poor condition and invest to meet housing needs. There is an increased emphasis on local decision-making based on assessments of local needs for all forms of housing, and on long-term local housing strategies drawn up by authorities in partnership with communities and integrated with other objectives and programmes.

7.48 Local housing strategies should look at problems of poor condition and social exclusion in existing stock, and the scope for making better use of empty or under-utilised homes, as well as the need for new housing. They should also set housing in wider contexts which take account of local employment opportunities, health services, schools, and crime. This is the approach taken by the Single Regeneration Budget and the New Deal for Communities.

7.49 As required by the Home Energy Conservation Act 1995 (HECA), local authorities are also implementing measures to improve significantly the energy efficiency of all residential accommodation their area. By integrating energy efficiency with other programmes covering issues such as health, education and the environment, local authorities can deliver improvements in line with their wider interest in local sustainability issues.

Fuel poverty

Over 4.3 million households in England are "fuel poor", spending 10% or more of their income on keeping warm. Nearly 800,000 of them need to spend 20% or more.[10]

Following the Comprehensive Spending Review, £375 million will be spent between 1999 and 2002 on programmes directly targeted at fuel poverty. The target is to install energy efficiency measures in 1 million buildings by 2002. The Government is also reviewing its overall fuel poverty policy, and will consult on proposals this Spring.

Most of the extra resources being made available for housing more generally are expected to be invested in stock refurbishment, complementing fuel poverty programmes and delivering additional improvements in energy efficiency.

7.50 The Government is working to improve housing management and ensure that tenants are fully involved in decisions. It has consulted on a Best Value framework for housing (see para 7.80), and on proposals to introduce Tenant Participation Compacts in every local authority by April 2000.

7.51 The Empty Homes Agency is funded by Government to work with local authorities to tackle the problems of vacant housing and to convert disused commercial property for residential use. Policy Action Teams established following the Social Exclusion Unit's report on neighbourhood renewal will make recommendations for tackling the problems of unpopular housing and for raising standards of housing management.

7.52 The Government has launched a new initiative to improve the quality of housing, with the publication of a set of Housing Quality Indicators. These allow designers to evaluate aspects such as internal and external layout, space standards, construction and energy efficiency. Initially, they will be used for new publicly funded housing schemes but they will be tested to assess their potential for use across new and existing stock in both public and private sectors.

9   Local Authority Housing Investment Programme: Operational Information Returns to DETR, 1998.

10 Details in the Government's consultation paper on fuel poverty policy, 11 May 1999.

Key actions and commitments

- Health White Paper targets

- Integrated transport policy: Commission for Integrated Transport to advise on future targets for public transport and road traffic

- Fuel poverty strategy consultation in Spring 1999; energy efficiency measures to be installed in 1 million buildings by 2002

- Major investment in housing; local authority housing strategies to incorporate sustainable development objectives

Indicators

Expected years of healthy life (headline)

Health inequalities

Health indicators on heart disease and strokes, cancer, accidents and mental health

Respiratory illness

Hospital waiting lists

Road traffic (headline)

Average journey length by purpose

Passenger travel by mode

Traffic congestion

Distance travelled relative to income

How children get to school

People finding access difficult

Access for the disabled (to be developed)

Access to rural services

Participation in sport and cultural activities

Homes judged unfit to live in (headline)

Temporary accommodation

Fuel poverty

7.53   Later this year, the Government will publish a Housing Policy Green Paper, aimed at ensuring that everyone has the opportunity of a decent home.

Shaping our surroundings

7.54   Attractive streets and buildings, low levels of traffic, noise and pollution, green spaces, and community safety, are fundamental to a good quality of life whether in city, town, or village. Failure to address these issues, or to accommodate change, can lead to long-term decline.

7.55   We also need to consider the role of cities, towns and villages within wider regions. New developments must be planned in ways which revitalise our urban areas, ensure thriving rural communities, conserve the historic environment and maintain the character of our townscapes and countryside.

Thriving neighbourhoods are essential to quality of life

BETTER PLANNING AND DESIGN

7.56   Many respondents to *Opportunities for change* and to the consultation exercise carried out by the Government's Urban Task Force identified neighbourhoods with easy access to services and a mix of uses as the basis for sustainable communities of the future. In order to create more sustainable patterns of development, we need to:

- concentrate the majority of new development within existing urban areas;

7.67 Initiatives such as Community Forests, the Central Scotland Forest and the Amman Gwendraeth initiative in the Welsh valleys are creating new woodlands, delivering access, recreation, land reclamation, education and biodiversity benefits in and around towns and cities.

Development should take account of history and landscape

7.68 The Government will issue guidance for local authorities on ways of using trees and forestry in regeneration and improvement, particularly of urban and surrounding areas. It will also promote better care of existing urban trees through advice and information, supported by research.

7.69 Starting later this year, the National Lottery New Opportunities Fund's *Green Spaces and Sustainable Communities* initiative will provide grants for local environmental improvement, including through community groups.

7.70 We also need to reinforce local distinctiveness and heritage. This means conservation and re-use of existing buildings, and ensuring that development takes account of history and landscape. While not all the historic environment can be kept unchanged, we need to look for opportunities to conserve local heritage in ways which make good use of physical resources and contribute to economic and social objectives: for example by re-using historic buildings for housing, business premises, community space, or tourism.

7.71 Business, local authorities, tourism and conservation bodies can work in partnership – for example, through Heritage Economic Regeneration Schemes, part of English Heritage's new strategy for conservation-led regeneration. Grants are also available through the Heritage Lottery Fund's Urban Parks Programme and Townscape Heritage Initiative.

7.72 Where areas are already of high quality, careful management is needed – for example, to guard against inappropriate new development or to manage the impacts of tourism. Properly managed and developed, tourism can underpin economic activity, support services, and assist conservation and enhancement of the local environment. The new national body for tourism in England and regional tourist boards will promote development of visitor management plans.

Heritage and Regeneration

Baltic Flour Mill, Gateshead
English Partnerships has invested £4.7 million to convert a disused flour mill on the south bank of the River Tyne into a contemporary art gallery, in partnership with Gateshead Metropolitan Borough Council, Northern Arts and the private sector. The development is helping to attract private sector development to the south bank of the river.

Lauderdale House, Dunbar, East Lothian
This was a prominent, but derelict, 18th Century building in Dunbar town centre. It now provides 27 homes for single people, the elderly and families. A flagship for the Dunbar Initiative, the project was supported by Scottish Homes, Historic Scotland, the local authority, the local enterprise company and Scottish Power, as well as private finance.

7.73 The Government will be working to develop indicators to measure conservation of the entire historic environment. In the meantime, an indicator of listed buildings at risk of decay will be included in the national set of sustainable development indicators.

In June 1997, the Prime Minister set a target for all local communities to have such strategies in place by 2000. The Government and the Local Government Management Board (now the Improvement and Development Agency) have published guidance on these strategies[14] and are developing in consultation with the Local Government Association a core menu of indicators which local authorities could use. These will be closely linked to the headline indicators and the indicators to be used in national reporting.

Local Agenda 21 Strategies

A Vision for Vale Royal, Cheshire, was developed by a partnership between the local council and other groups and drew in as many local people as possible. It includes action points for all sectors of the community, from local authorities to individuals.

Follow-up is underway in several smaller communities. In Weaverham, a "Millennium ream Party" was attended by more than 1 in 5 useholds, who said what they wanted for the re of their village. As a result, many actions aking place, ranging from eco-audits of ls and pubs, to a local skills directory, better bles and the opening of a parish office.

Government will give local authorities to promote the economic, social and tal well-being of their areas. Authorities ted to weigh up the impact of their the overall well-being of the area and who live and work there. To provide nce in the delivery of services, be expected to work with other ary bodies and local communities rehensive strategies for promoting community strategies may l Agenda 21 strategies, or ide to integrate the two. Local s should also inform all other and programmes, including local The new duty on authorities to he delivery of services will

stimulate new ways to carry out their functions in line with sustainable development objectives.

7.81 At regional level in England, sustainable development will have a place in all strategic documents produced by public bodies. In addition, the Government wishes to see high level sustainable development frameworks for each English region by the end of 2000. Progress has already been made in some areas, such as the North West, where a strategy has been issued for consultation.

7.82 The regional frameworks should draw on this Strategy and on Local Agenda 21 work in the region. They should identify regional needs and priorities, preferably based on regional indicators, and provide a sustainable development context for other regional initiatives. The Government will issue guidance on the content and preparation of the frameworks.

7.83 Regional frameworks will not be statutory, and their success will depend on the commitment of organisations across the region. They will need to have the support of a wide range of stakeholders, and should be agreed by Regional Chambers[15] (groupings of local authorities and other regional partners). Detailed arrangements for their production will need to be worked out at regional level, taking account of progress already made: the work might be led by a round table set up for the purpose or by a Regional Chamber.

7.84 The Government is also consulting on proposals to improve the preparation and content of Regional Planning Guidance[16], which sets a long-term spatial framework for future development in English regions. Among its proposals are that a sustainability appraisal should be undertaken of the environmental, economic and social impacts of development options, for the start of the preparation process. The Government will publish good practice guidance on how to undertake such an appraisal.

7.85 The Government's modernisation of the planning system will help to achieve a system which is fair, open and operated by democratically

munities for the 21st Century. Why and how to prepare an effective Local Agenda 21 strategy. uary 1998

designated under the Regional Development Act 1998.

Note 11: Regional Planning public consultation draft. February 1999. DETR. C8650.

REDUCING CRIME AND THE FEAR OF CRIME

7.74 Everyone has a right to live in a community that is safe. Crime reinforces social exclusion and decline. It makes people reluctant to walk or to take public transport. It imposes economic costs. There has been a long-term rise in crime, although some offences have declined in recent years. Much acquisitive crime, such as shoplifting and burglary, is committed by drug misusing offenders to feed their habits. Fear of crime is common, particularly among women – over a quarter are very worried about physical attack.

7.75 The Crime and Disorder Act 1998 requires local authorities and police in England and Wales to implement strategies to reduce crime and disorder. In doing so, they must work in partnership with other local organisations and consult widely with the local community. A new £250 million crime reduction programme was announced in July 1998, including pilot projects targeted at families, children and schools, burglary, targeted policing, sentencing, crime-resistant products, and reducing the risk of re-offending.

7.76 Overall policies on regeneration, planning, transport and social exclusion will all play a part in reducing crime. Community safety is emphasised in programmes such as the Single Regeneration Budget and Safer Cities. The Government's transport policy addresses the particular needs for safer public transport for women, older people and ethnic minorities.

Key actions and commitments

- 60% of new housing in England on previously developed sites by 2008

- New Opportunities Fund *Green Spaces and Sustainable Communities* initiative

- Local authorities to implement crime and disorder strategies

Indicators

Household and population growth

New homes built on previously developed land (headline)

Retail floorspace in town centres and out of t

Vacant land and properties and derelict lar

Noise levels

Quality of surroundings

Access to local green space (to be

Buildings of Grade I and II* at

Level of crime (headline)

Fear of crime

Bringing it
integrated
stronger

7.77 To ma
sustainabl
policies
to susta

7.78
the
d

7.80 The
a new duty
environme
will be expe
decisions on
on the peopl
greater cohere
authorities wil
agencies, volun
to develop com
well-being. Such
complement Loca
authorities may de
Agenda 21 strategi
local plans, policies
development plans.
obtain Best Value in

14 Sustainable local com
DETR/LGA/LGMB, Ja
15 The Regional Chamber
16 Planning Policy Guidand

accountable bodies; a planning system which is an active force for change, rather than simply reacting to events. In February 1999, a new policy concordat between central and local government in England was published. It sets out basic principles against which the planning system needs to operate, including achieving sustainable development, delivering best value and co-ordinating with other policy areas.

7.86 The Government's commitment to integrated policy making for sustainable development is also reflected in specific initiatives:

- The forthcoming Urban White Paper in England will set out a framework to secure an urban renaissance, based on towns and cities which are pleasant, liveable places with all in the community having the opportunity to prosper and realise their full potential. The planning of towns and cities will be a strong theme of the Paper, which will draw on the recommendations of the Urban Task Force led by Lord Rogers.

- The Rural White Paper in England will set out the framework for a living and working countryside, based on thriving communities with a balanced mix of businesses, jobs and homes, and good access to services for all, and ensuring access so that the countryside can be enjoyed by all. The Urban and Rural White Papers will be complementary, taking account of the relationships between rural and urban areas and providing a basis for better integration between them.

- In Wales, work is underway on urban and rural issues in preparation for the National Assembly, including work by the Rural Partnership in Wales on a rural development agenda. The European Structural Funds Task Force is also preparing an integrated National Development Strategy.

- Research in six key areas of England will build on local experience to develop best practice in managing and co-ordinating initiatives such as New Deal for Communities, the reshaped Single Regeneration Budget, Health and Education Action Zones and Employment Zones.

- Partnership between regional and local tiers is important. A Policy Action Team is looking at how to link local authority plans upwards to regional and national strategies and downwards to neighbourhood level. Guidance to the RDAs stresses the need to work closely with local authorities, and encourages RDAs to take account of other regional and local plans, including Local Agenda 21 strategies.

Involving everyone

7.87 Public involvement is essential for a truly sustainable community. It is a major theme running through the Government's modernising agenda for local government, and policies on regeneration and social exclusion.

LOCAL GOVERNMENT AND PARTICIPATION

7.88 Voting in local elections is one way for people to have their say. Low voting figures are a symptom of a lack of faith in local democracy. To rectify that, the Government's White Paper, *Modern local government: in touch with the people*, outlined aims for modernising local democracy.[17] Guidance on enhancing public participation in local government was published in October 1998.

7.89 Most Local Agenda 21 processes are led by the local authority, with broad involvement by other local groups. Some councils have gone further, with community groups taking a lead role in drawing up a strategy. Experience with Local Agenda 21 will help local authorities in developing consultation arrangements under Best Value and other local initiatives.

7.90 The Government's aims for modernising planning include the need to make development plans shorter and clearer and for consultation on plans to be better targeted. Implicit within this is the need for consultation with all stakeholders, including the public, and to increase public knowledge of the planning process. This is reflected in the new guidance in England on development plans.[18]

---

17 *Modern local government: in touch with the people.* July 1998, Cm 4014. ISBN 0 10 140142 6.

18 As set out in the consultation draft of Planning Policy Guidance note 12.

7.91 There are many other opportunities to promote involvement in shaping communities. For example, the Environment Agency's system of Local Environment Agency Plans provide opportunities for stakeholders to participate in developing an environmental strategy for local areas, taking account of economic and social needs. The Environment Agency has also issued new proposals for consultation on contentious licence decisions.

COMMUNITY ACTION AND INVOLVEMENT

7.92 Effective participation involves all sectors of society. The modernising local government agenda recognises that ethnic minorities in particular are often under-represented in local decision making and a Local Agenda 21 Round Table report highlighted that their participation in specific sustainable development activities has been relatively low.[19] This may be because of language or cultural barriers to involvement, which need to be identified and broken down, or because of different cultural perspectives on sustainable development.

7.93 More generally, race equality is high on the Government agenda. It is working towards an inclusive society where everyone, regardless of race or religion, has equal rights, opportunities and responsibilities – while being able to maintain their own culture, traditions, language and values.

7.94 Capacity building and strengthened local partnerships are features of the Single Regeneration Budget and the New Deal for Communities. The New Deal for Communities will involve participation of local people from development to implementation, to ensure partnerships are rooted in local communities and deliver lasting change, beyond the lifetime of the regeneration scheme itself.

7.95 Voluntary and community activity can do much to promote social inclusion and cohesion in a community, with benefits for the recipients, participants and society as a whole. The Prime Minister wants to see a greater involvement by everyone in community life. He has challenged

people in Britain to mark the Millennium with an 'explosion in giving'.

7.96 The key aim of the Prime Minister's initiative is to help build a sense of community by encouraging and supporting all forms of community involvement. It will involve strengthening people's desire to get involved, making it easier for them to do so, and encouraging more and higher quality opportunities for involvement. Demonstration projects will be established across the country this year, via the Home Office Active Community Unit and local partnerships, to test imaginative new ways of bringing together volunteers and volunteering opportunities.

7.97 In the most deprived areas, levels of voluntary activity tend to be very low – around 7% compared with around 20% in more affluent communities. The Government is looking at how to encourage the number, range and vitality of community groups in such areas. In doing so, it will consult widely. Community involvement is at the heart of the National Lottery New Opportunities Fund's *Green Spaces and Sustainable Communities* initiative, which will have a particular focus on deprived areas.

People need the chance to play their part in shaping change

7.98 In addition, the Government's Compact with the voluntary sector[20] sets out its commitment to working in partnership with the voluntary sector and provides a framework to help guide the

19 Local Agenda 21 Roundtable Guidance Note 14, LGMB, 1997.

20 *Getting it right together*, the Compact on relations between Government and the Voluntary & Community Sector in England. CM4100, Home Office November 1998. ISBN 0 10 141002 6.

relationship at every level. It recognises the vital role of voluntary and community organisations in enabling individuals in all parts of society to contribute to the development of their communities. Similar Compacts have been agreed in Scotland, Wales and Northern Ireland.

Volunteering and Sustainable Development

Residents, trained and facilitated by the British Trust for Conservation Volunteers, created Studley Estate Community Garden, Lambeth as part of a programme designed to reduce crime, build community infrastructure, provide training for residents, and promote networking between community groups, as well as to create an urban wildlife habitat.

7.99 Access to justice for all is an essential part of building sustainable communities. Under new Civil Procedure Rules introduced by the Government, civil justice will be simpler, cheaper and more expeditious. These Rules have the overriding objective of enabling the courts to deal with cases justly. Courts will be required to manage cases actively, including encouraging the parties to use an alternative dispute resolution procedure, if appropriate, and facilitating the use of such procedure. Plans for a Community Legal Service, and the wider availability of conditional fee arrangements will also promote improved access to justice.

Key actions and commitments

- Urban and Rural White Papers

- Regional frameworks for sustainable development in English regions by 2000

- New planning guidance on regional and local plans to promote sustainable development

- Co-ordination of regeneration and employment policies through New Deals and Zones

- Strengthened local partnerships and capacity building through Single Regeneration Budget and New Deal for Communities

- Increasing public participation in local democracy

- Government Compact with the voluntary sector

Indicators

Number of local authorities with LA 21 plans

Community spirit (to be developed)

Voluntary activity (to be developed)

CHAPTER 8

Managing the Environment and Resources

Major environmental and resource challenges which the UK faces are:

- achieving major long-term cuts in greenhouse gas emissions whilst ensuring secure, diverse supplies of energy at competitive prices in environmentally-acceptable ways;

- improving the quality of our air;

- safeguarding freshwater resources and water quality, at a time when pressures from climate change and household demand are likely to increase;

- safeguarding the health and productivity of the seas around our shores;

- minimising the loss of our soil resource, and maintaining and enhancing soil quality;

- reversing trends of damage to our landscape and wildlife;

- reducing the spread of persistent or diffuse pollutants and improving management of waste;

- working with others to combat global challenges such as climate change and threats to biodiversity, oceans and forests.

8.1 In the UK, increasing prosperity has meant that in many ways the environment has improved. The smogs of the 1950s are gone. River quality has risen in the last decade. The UK does not face the severe pollution problems found elsewhere, particularly in some developing countries.

8.2 But challenges remain. We have to work with others to address global problems, so that environmental limits are not breached and valuable resources are not destroyed: for example, avoiding dangerous climate change, or severe declines in fish stocks. Domestically, environmental damage still reduces quality of life: air pollution harms our health; and people are justifiably concerned over declines in wildlife, such as lower numbers of farmland birds. New challenges are emerging, such as the potential impacts of certain chemicals.

An integrated approach

8.3 The Government's approach is based on:

- achieving **overall improvements in environmental quality** and, where overall standards are already relatively good, ensuring that they do not slip back;

- ensuring **continued productivity of renewable resources** and, while making prudent use of non-renewable resources, encouraging alternatives for the longer term;

- achieving environmental improvements in ways which **reinforce economic and social objectives**, such as better health, more efficient use of energy, or competitiveness;

- **acting proportionately**: recognising that not every environmental improvement will be justifiable when all sustainable development objectives are taken into account.

8.4 The Government's record on environmental protection is strong: this chapter refers to many initiatives already taken. But this Strategy is not the place to set out all of these in full – any more than it is the place for a comprehensive account of policies on health, transport or competitiveness.

8.5   We need to consider impacts on air, land and water, and ensure that solving one problem does not create another. The system of Integrated Pollution Control for industrial processes is based on this approach, and allows environmental impacts to be regulated in a way which is more efficient for industry and its regulators. Its forthcoming replacement by Integrated Pollution Prevention and Control will reinforce these benefits. For other decisions, the idea of 'Best Practicable Environmental Option' (BPEO), originally recommended by the Royal Commission on Environmental Pollution and introduced by the Government, can help to identify options.[1]

Key actions and commitments

- Initiatives on climate change, air quality, water, wildlife and other issues identified in this chapter

- New chemicals strategy

- Implement new Integrated Pollution Prevention and Control legislation

Indicators

Concentrations of persistent organic pollutants (to be developed)

Dangerous substances in water

Other indicators set out elsewhere in this chapter are also relevant

---

8.6   Pollutants can move between soil, air and water. Some are released as products are used: as car tyres wear out or as pesticides are applied. Such dispersed releases are especially important when pollutants build up in the environment, either because they accumulate in the bodies of people or animals or in plants, or because they persist for long periods. We must not store up problems for the future: the forthcoming chemicals strategy will set

down guidelines on the place of precautionary action in controls on chemicals. It will outline the UK's view on how to improve and speed up the European programme of environmental risk assessments and encourage the chemical industries to take more responsibility for assessing and reducing environmental impact.

8.7   At present, there is a particular concern about 'endocrine disrupters' – chemicals which mimic hormones. The UK is working with other countries to gauge the extent of any problems. Particular global attention has also focused on persistent organic pollutants, on which the UK is playing a leading role to secure a global treaty by 2000.

Climate change and energy supply

8.8   Climate change is a great threat to global sustainable development. Globally, 1998 was the hottest year since instrumental records began in 1860 and seven out of the last ten years have been the hottest on record. Some climate change is now inevitable, and we will have to adapt to that. But climate change must be kept within limits which global society can accommodate. Exactly what those may be needs to be defined, but action is likely to involve reducing global and UK greenhouse gas emissions, over time, to significantly below today's levels.

In the long term more energy will need to come from energy sources which emit little or no CO_2

---

1   The Royal Commission on Environmental Pollution stated that 'a BPEO is the outcome of a systematic and consultative decision making procedure which emphasises the protection and conservation of the environment across land, air and water. The BPEO procedure establishes, for a given set of objectives, the option that provides the most benefits or the least damage to the environment as a whole, at acceptable cost, in the long term as well as in the short term'.

8.9   Achieving this as living standards rise, in the UK and globally, will require significant changes in the way energy is produced and used. It will require policies which meet the needs of people and businesses for affordable energy, warmth and mobility, and ensure secure and diverse energy supplies in environmentally-acceptable ways.

REDUCING EMISSIONS

8.10 In Kyoto in 1997, developed countries agreed to reduce their emissions of a 'basket' of six greenhouse gases by just over 5.2% below 1990 levels over the period 2008-2012. The EU agreed to an 8% reduction, which was subsequently shared between member states: the UK agreed to contribute a reduction of 12.5%. An action plan to agree the outstanding issues from Kyoto was agreed in Buenos Aires in November 1998.

8.11 In October 1998, the Government launched a consultation on how to meet the 12.5% target and how to move towards its domestic goal of a 20% reduction in carbon dioxide emissions by 2010, in ways which enhance competitiveness and promote social inclusion[2]. The Government intends to publish a draft UK Climate Change Programme later in 1999 and to put the final programme in place in good time for ratification of the Kyoto Protocol. Initiatives described elsewhere in this Strategy will contribute to the Programme: on transport policy; greater energy efficiency; improved technology; and sustainable forestry.

8.12 Further cuts in emissions will be needed in the longer term. Meeting the challenges beyond 2010 is likely to entail:

- significant changes in energy production;

- cutting road traffic emissions through more fuel efficient vehicles and reducing people's need to travel by car;

- big improvements in the energy efficiency of industrial processes, homes, offices, and appliances, and changes in behaviour to promote more efficient use.

CHANGES IN ENERGY SUPPLY

8.13 In the 1990s, primarily due to market liberalisation, the UK shifted from carbon-intensive fuels such as coal and oil towards less carbon-intensive fuels such as gas and nuclear energy. This reduced carbon dioxide emissions, but the changes were caused in part by market distortions which also failed to reflect wider economic and social impacts. Following its *Review of Energy Sources for Power Generation*, the Government is removing these distortions.[3] As a result, in the short term, the shift towards lower emission fuels will be less pronounced.

8.14 In the longer term, more energy will have to come from energy sources which emit little or no carbon dioxide, in particular from new and renewable sources. In September 1998, the Government

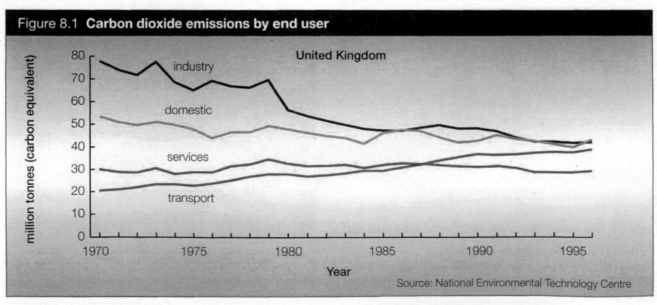

Figure 8.1 **Carbon dioxide emissions by end user**

United Kingdom

y-axis: million tonnes (carbon equivalent)
x-axis: Year

Lines: industry, domestic, services, transport

Source: National Environmental Technology Centre

2   *UK Climate Change Programme – a consultation paper.* October 1998, DETR. 98EP0136.

3   *Conclusions of the review of energy sources for power generation and Government response to the 4th and 5th reports of the Trade and Industry Committee.* October 1998, Cm 4071. ISBN 0 10 140712 2.

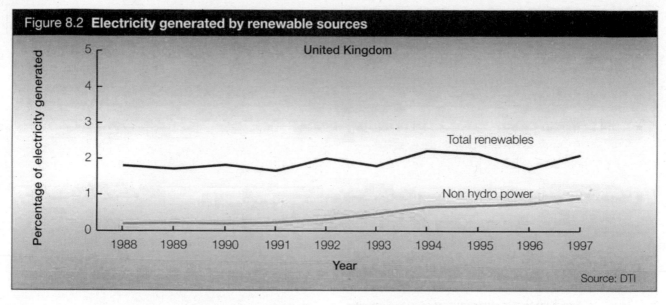

Figure 8.2 **Electricity generated by renewable sources**

United Kingdom

Total renewables

Non hydro power

Percentage of electricity generated

Year

Source: DTI

launched the largest ever package of support under the Non-Fossil Fuel Obligation for renewable electricity sources. These measures should lead to 5% of UK electricity being supplied by renewables by 2003, up from 2% now. Earlier this year the Government published a consultation document on future renewable energy policy.[4] The Government intends working towards a target of 10% of UK electricity being supplied by renewable energy, cost effectively, as soon as possible. It hopes to achieve this by 2010.

8.15 All forms of electricity generation have some environmental impacts. So a shift towards renewables does not mean halting the search for energy efficiency. Nor does it mean ceasing to use the UK's fossil fuel resources, provided exploitation is managed in an environmentally acceptable way. Fossil fuels are bound to play a large part in energy generation for many years to come as we move towards new forms of energy production, and managing the UK's resources can help to ensure security of supply, as well as economic and social benefits.

8.16 Nuclear energy is generated without direct production of carbon dioxide. But the cost of building nuclear power stations is high and there is no strong economic case for new build. Radioactive waste also has to be disposed of safely. There is presently no disposal route for intermediate and high level radioactive waste and so it has to be stored. The Government will issue a consultation paper on radioactive waste management towards the end of 1999. It is likely that nuclear power's contribution to reducing emissions will decrease in the first decades of the 21st century as existing capacity is retired.

ADAPTING TO CLIMATE CHANGE

8.17 The world already faces temperature increases which will result in changed weather patterns and higher sea levels – affecting food and water supplies for millions of people, threatening coastal settlements, and allowing diseases like malaria to spread. In the UK, there may be more droughts in the south and east, more flooding in the north and west, more storm damage, threats to the coast and agricultural land, and changes in wildlife and habitats. The UK Climate Impacts Programme has been set up to help the public and private sectors assess their vulnerability to such changes and to develop adaptation strategies. Climate change scenarios for the UK were published in October 1998 and are available to help decision makers assess their vulnerability to climate change.

HELPING DEVELOPING COUNTRIES

8.18 As developing countries' economies grow, they will need to develop ways to curb their own emissions. The Government will help them do so, for instance through promotion of energy management practices and low emission technologies. Since 1992, the UK has committed £670 million to such projects: examples are restructuring the state-owned power sector in India, stimulating a market for wind-pumps in China, and promoting energy efficient woodstoves. It has also contributed £215 million to the Global Environment Facility, which helps developing countries to meet the extra initial capital costs of reducing emissions.

4   *New and Renewable Energy – Prospects for the 21st Century* DTI, March 1999.

Key actions and commitments

- internationally agreed target to reduce UK emissions of greenhouse gases by 12.5% below 1990 levels by 2008–2012;

- aim to move towards domestic goal of a 20% reduction in carbon dioxide emissions below 1990 levels by 2010

- existing measures likely to deliver 5% of electricity generation from renewables by 2003; consultation on future policy under way;

- UK Climate Impacts Programme to develop strategies for adaptation to climate change.

Indicators

Emissions of greenhouse gases (headline)

Rise in global temperature

Sea level rise

Carbon dioxide emissions by end user

Depletion of fossil fuels

Electricity from renewable sources

Discharges from the nuclear industry

Radioactive waste stocks

Air and Atmosphere

8.19 The Government's air quality policy aims to ensure that polluting emissions do not cause harm to human health or the environment. Such harm brings social and economic costs, with burdens often falling on inner city residents who face general problems of degraded local environments. But people in rural areas are also affected, as well as forests, lakes, crops, wildlife and buildings.

LOCAL AIR QUALITY

8.20 The headline indicator of air quality measures the days on which air pollution exceeds levels at which, experts advise, there could be harm to human health. On average, these levels are exceeded on more than one day in ten. This is too often, and the Government has set demanding 5-10 year objectives for a range of pollutants which will reduce the number of exceedences.

8.21 The specific pollutants responsible for problems vary. In towns and cities, air pollution is a mixture of gases and particles; in rural areas it is often low-level ozone. Transport and industry are a major cause of both.

8.22 The Government is consulting on proposals to tighten objectives for five of the eight pollutants in the National Air Quality Strategy: benzene, 1,3-butadiene, carbon monoxide, lead and nitrogen dioxide (hourly objective only).[5] The Government proposes to leave the annual nitrogen dioxide objective unchanged and review in 2000 the measures needed and the feasibility of achieving both the annual and the hourly objectives. The objectives for ozone and sulphur dioxide are to remain as they are; that for particles is to be replaced with provisional limit values in EU legislation. The review is assisted by the Air Quality Forum, whose members come from local government, business, the voluntary sector and health groups.

8.23 Action by everyone is important:

- local authorities have a duty to assess air quality in their areas and, if air quality objectives are unlikely to be achieved with current measures, designate air quality management areas and produce action plans;

- scientists and industry can develop technology and skills needed for cleaner air and increased prosperity;

- individuals have an impact through decisions on the type of car they buy, car use and domestic heating.

8.24 The Government's integrated transport policy has a big part to play. Measures to reduce emissions from individual vehicles are also important. So are integrated pollution control policies and planning policies which minimise industrial pollution and avoid damage to sensitive locations, and which use

5   *Review of the National Air Quality Strategy: proposals to amend the strategy.* January 1999, DETR. 98EP0541/A.

planning conditions to reduce pollution or its effects. As a result emissions from road transport in urban areas are set to fall by half in the ten years to 2005. Emissions from industry are also set to fall. For instance, emissions of sulphur dioxide from the electricity supply industry are expected to fall by more than half from 1998 to 2005.

8.25 The analysis of existing and proposed measures suggests that action already taken or proposed to improve air quality in the UK will generate significant health and non-health benefits. For example, the total number of deaths brought forward by air pollution in the UK is expected to fall by approximately 18,500 between 1996 and 2005.

Key measures to reduce pollution from transport

- the EU Auto Oil programme will mean cleaner petrol and diesel and significantly tighter emission standards for new vehicles from 2000, and further improvements in 2005;

- banning of general sale of leaded petrol from 1 January 2000;

- different rates of duty to encourage greater use of cleaner fuels;

- annual increases in fuel duty of at least 6% in real terms;

- vehicle excise duty concessions of up to £1000 for the cleanest lorries and buses from March 1999.

INTERNATIONAL ACTION

8.26 In the EU and internationally, the Government presses for emission reductions based on sound science and a thorough assessment of all the costs and benefits. The Government supports the long term EU goal of not exceeding 'critical loads' for acidification – levels of pollutant deposition below which significant harmful effects to the environment do not occur.

8.27 The Government supports a gradual movement towards this goal, which could not be achieved quickly without unacceptable social or economic impacts, in this country and elsewhere. Current commitments will reduce significantly the areas of the UK at risk from acid rain by 2010, and the Government is pressing for further development of ambitious, but achievable, international agreements. Levels of sulphur dioxide and nitrogen oxides are already falling.

OZONE LAYER

8.28 The Government supports a proposed EU regulation which will introduce more stringent controls on ozone depleting substances. For example, it will impose a general ban on the supply and use of chlorofluorocarbons with only a few limited exceptions. Significant progress has already been made to protect the ozone layer under the Montreal Protocol, the international agreement which controls the production and consumption of ozone depleting substances. If all countries meet

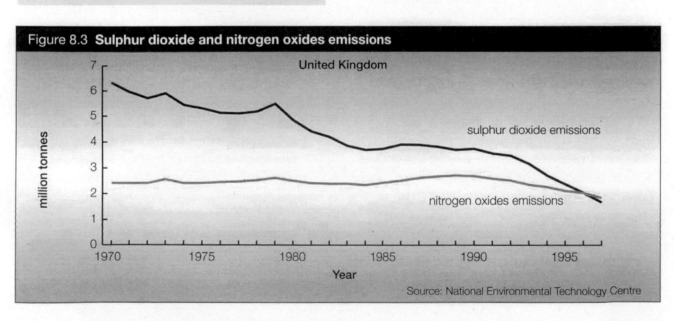

Figure 8.3 **Sulphur dioxide and nitrogen oxides emissions**

United Kingdom

sulphur dioxide emissions

nitrogen oxides emissions

million tonnes

Year

Source: National Environmental Technology Centre

their obligations, the ozone layer is expected to recover fully by the middle of the 21st century.

Freshwater

8.29 Water is a renewable resource, vital for public health and the environment. Safeguarding resources and ensuring affordable supplies are essential for sustainable development. The UK does not face severe problems of water availability and quality but there are marked regional variations and many pressures. Demand is likely to grow, largely due to increased household use. Parts of the country, notably the south and east, already appear to be experiencing changed weather patterns. New development and urbanisation

increase demand and create further pollution pressures. Diffuse inputs, such as run off and leaching from roads, agricultural land and urban areas, loss of habitats and pressure on groundwaters all present substantial challenges.

8.30 The Government's policy response to these challenges started with the Water Summit it held in May 1997. It includes:

- **Integrated management of river catchments,** considering environmental quality alongside the needs of homes, industry, agriculture and other uses of watercourses, and planning of land use and development. In England and Wales this approach is consolidated in Local Environment Agency Plans, with informal arrangements in Scotland and Northern Ireland. It will be reinforced by the proposed EU Water Framework Directive.

- **Improving river quality.** Nearly 95% of monitored river length is of good or fair quality. But river quality objectives along almost a fifth of river length in England and Wales are not met, and there are increasing pressures on some waters of highest quality which support the richest biodiversity. The Government aims to eliminate half of that shortfall by 2005, with further improvements in compliance in the longer term.

- **Water resource planning.** All water companies in England and Wales have to produce 25-year resource plans, agreed with the Environment Agency and kept under annual review. The plans must take a precautionary approach to demand management and must include proposals for resource development – subject to full appraisal – if projected demand cannot reasonably and reliably be met from existing sources.[6] Revised guidance to local authorities in England on the implications of new development for resource planning has been incorporated in consultation draft planning guidance by the Government.[7] In Scotland, the Secretary of State and the water authorities have a duty to promote conservation and effective use of water resources and adequate

6 *Maintaining Public Water Supplies.* DETR and Welsh Office, January 1999.

7 Revision of Planning Policy Guidance Note 12 – Development Plans. Public consultation draft, DETR, February 1999.

supplies. There are sufficient resources to meet average demands in Scotland until at least 2016.[8]

- **Avoiding waste of water.** About 25% of the public water supply in England and Wales is lost through leakage. Mandatory leakage targets for companies have been set which will reduce leakage between 1996/97 and 2000 by 26%. Tougher regulations for water efficiency of equipment and fittings are being introduced. In Scotland, the water authorities are expected to seek reductions in leakage wherever economically justified. The Environment Technology Best Practice Programme will continue to promote water saving in industry, and *Are you doing your bit?* will provide information on what individuals can do.

- **A fair charging system.** Some people have argued for higher water prices, combined with metering, to control demand and to reflect environmental costs of water use. But people and firms must be able to afford the water they need, and families should face neither hardship because of water bills nor disconnection. The Government does not favour universal compulsory metering and aims to deliver cuts in average water prices in England and Wales over the next few years, coupled with substantial investment to deliver improvements in water quality. Companies in England and Wales have been asked to develop charging regimes which distinguish between water used for essential and

About 25% of public water supply in England is lost through leakage

for discretionary purposes. In Scotland, water charges must be approved by the independent Scottish Water and Sewerage Customers Council, or by Ministers if agreement between the Customers Council and water authorities cannot be reached.

- **Maintaining the high quality of drinking water.** Drinking water quality in the UK is generally high. Standards for lead, and controls to prevent contamination with cryptosporidium, are being reinforced under a precautionary approach to safeguarding human health. The 1998 Groundwater Regulations should ensure that pollution of groundwater by pesticides and other dangerous substances is prevented.

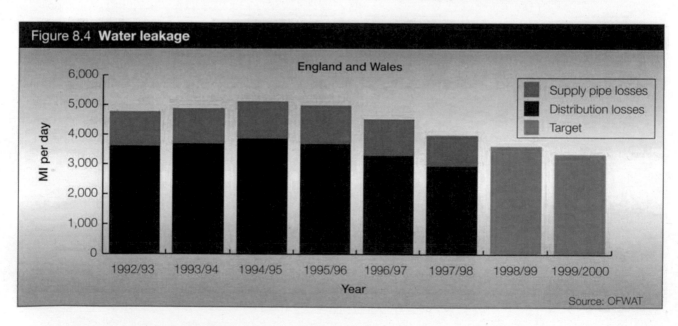

Figure 8.4 Water leakage

England and Wales

Legend:
- Supply pipe losses
- Distribution losses
- Target

Y-axis: Ml per day (0 to 6,000)
X-axis: Year (1992/93, 1993/94, 1994/95, 1995/96, 1996/97, 1997/98, 1998/99, 1999/2000)

Source: OFWAT

8 *Public Water Supplies in Scotland: An Assessment of Demands and Resources at 1994.*
The Scottish Office ISBN 0 7480 7480.

- **Controlling abstractions.** The Government has announced changes to the water abstraction licensing system in England and Wales in order to protect the water environment whilst allowing properly-managed demand to be met.[9] Reviews are under way in Scotland and Northern Ireland.

- **Limiting pollution.** Secondary treatment will be normal by 2005 for all significant sewage discharges; higher treatment will be applied where required to remove nutrients or pathogens. A substantial programme will be implemented over the period to 2005 to improve unsatisfactory overflows from the sewerage system.

- **Protecting special sites.** The Government is taking steps to ensure that abstraction controls and discharge improvements play a full part in protecting the best wildlife and amenity sites.

Key actions and commitments

- Rivers of good or fair quality (headline)

- Water companies to reduce leakage by 26% by 2000 compared to 1996/97

- Real cuts in average prices for water consumers in England and Wales over next few years

- Changes to water abstraction licensing system

Indicators

Rivers of good or fair quality (headline)

Water demand and availability

Water affordability

Water leakage

Abstractions by purpose

Low flow in rivers (to be developed)

Nutrients in water

8.31 To help developing countries, the Government will expand support for integrated water management which helps the poor, for work to deal with problems such as arsenic contamination and salinated water sources, and for international organisations such as the Global Water Partnership. It has strongly supported a new European agreement on water-borne diseases, to be signed at the World Health Organisation's European Environment and Health Ministerial meeting in June 1999.

Seas, oceans and coasts

8.32 Seas and oceans are the major part of the planet that supports life, and drive the climate and the hydrological cycle. The UN Convention on the Law of the Sea, to which the UK is a party, provides a comprehensive framework for management of the oceans.

8.33 Many activities such as shipping, fishing, offshore minerals exploitation, coastal zone development, and land based activities make use of our seas and shores. We have to manage these activities to conserve the marine environment, while allowing sustainable use of marine resources and the passage of shipping.

8.34 In recent decades, global pressures on the marine environment have increased dramatically. Urgent international action to stop further degradation, and where necessary and feasible to reverse existing damage, is a priority. The Second London Oceans Workshop in December 1998 concluded that the two major problems were unsustainable fishing practices and pollution and other degradation from land based activities. These conclusions have been fed into the 1999 meeting of the UN Commission for Sustainable Development, which has oceans as one of its main topics.

---

9   *Taking Water Responsibly:* Government decisions following consultation on changes to the water abstraction licensing system in England and Wales. DETR and Welsh Office, March 1999.

QUALITY OF UK WATERS

8.35 The quality of UK coastal waters is generally good, with levels of contaminants unlikely to be a threat to marine life. Inputs of hazardous substances and nutrients are generally declining although hotspots of poor water quality exist. The Government and its partners in the OSPAR Commission for the Protection of the Marine Environment of the North East Atlantic have adopted a precautionary approach which aims to reduce or eliminate inputs of hazardous and radioactive substances of most concern as far as practicable by 2020. They have also agreed a strategy to control inputs of nutrients which disturb the balance of the marine environment. A quality assessment of the OSPAR area will be published in 2000 to inform future action.

8.36 Measures to improve river quality and limit emissions to air have a big part to play in reducing inputs, alongside measures on direct discharges to the sea. Secondary treatment will be the normal requirement for all sewage works making significant discharges to coastal waters.

8.37 Following substantial investment, almost 90% of UK bathing waters now comply with the European Bathing Waters Directive but performance is still too low in a few areas. The Government target is to raise consistent compliance with the Directive's mandatory standards to at least 97% by 2005 and to achieve a significant increase in compliance with its tougher guideline standards, particularly at major holiday resorts.

MANAGING MARINE ACTIVITIES

8.38 Most of the UK's trade goes by sea, and our waters are among the world's busiest. The Government has published a new strategy for sustainable shipping, which aims to increase skills, employment, and the UK's attractiveness to shipping enterprises. The Government is working to tighten international safety and environmental standards, where necessary, and to enhance compliance with these standards: for example, it has co-ordinated work within the International Maritime Organisation leading to a ban on discharges of oil from ships in north-west Europe. The dumping of sewage sludge at sea ended in 1998

and now only dredged material is routinely licensed for dumping. The Government continues to seek beneficial uses for dredged material to minimise the amount disposed at sea.

8.39 The UK is leading OSPAR work on a strategy to manage the environmental impacts of offshore oil and gas production. Environmental impact assessments are now required for all significant new UK oil and gas developments. In 1998, the Government agreed to an OSPAR ban on sea dumping of all steel off-shore oil and gas installations, thus promoting their reuse and recycling.

CONSERVING MARINE BIODIVERSITY

8.40 Protection of marine habitats and species is being given more attention. Under the UK Biodiversity Action Plan, plans for twelve marine habitats and sixteen marine species will be published by summer 1999. New measures to protect marine biodiversity were agreed in 1998 under the OSPAR Convention.

8.41 Coral is a good indicator of the quality of the marine environment and the impacts of global warming. The UK will support conservation of coral reefs through the International Coral Reef Initiative and support for the Global Coral Reef Monitoring Network.

FISHERIES

8.42 Fish is a valuable food resource, and the fishing industry remains an important source of jobs, often in areas remote from other sources of employment. Managed well, fish is a renewable resource; but stocks can be threatened by pollution and over-fishing. The latter is a serious problem, and not just in the UK. World fish catches have increased four fold since 1950. Thirteen out of fifteen of the world's main fisheries and many localised fisheries are under pressure. In some cases, recovery of stocks to commercial levels will be difficult to secure.

8.43 Assessments have been made of the minimum level of fish stocks necessary to enable fish to reproduce themselves. Currently these are known as

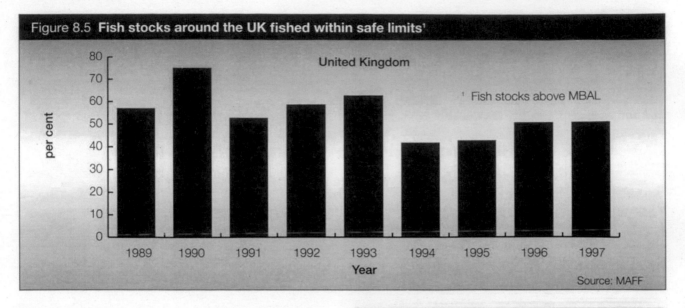

Figure 8.5 **Fish stocks around the UK fished within safe limits[1]**

United Kingdom

[1] Fish stocks above MBAL

per cent / Year

Source: MAFF

Minimum Biological Acceptable Levels (MBAL): in 1997, only 51% of stocks fished by EU fleets were above these levels. The International Council for the Exploration of the Sea is developing a new assessment framework, based on a precautionary approach.

8.44 The Government is committed to the sustainable management of fisheries through the European Union's Common Fisheries Policy (CFP). This means working to improve the management and conservation of fish stocks so that they are increasingly likely to be at levels above minimum safe limits. Unless we do that, we shall never provide a secure future for our fishing industry. To help the industry, the Government provides support through national and European grant schemes, including aid for processing and marketing, port facilities, vessel safety, fishery harbours, and restructuring and diversification of the industry in areas dependent on fisheries.

8.45 The Government will continue to press for improvements to the CFP. Its priorities include better enforcement, integrating environmental considerations more fully, effective controls on fishing effort, and improving the regional dimension of the CFP.

8.46 Over-fishing is a global problem. And some fishing vessels from the UK and other countries travel far afield for their catches. So action for sustainable fisheries needs international agreement. The UK will continue to work with other countries to achieve effective management and conservation of fish stocks, and to ensure that EU fisheries

Key actions and commitments

- Aim to reduce or eliminate inputs of hazardous and radioactive substances of most concern, as far as practicable, by 2020

- Aim for fish stocks above minimum levels necessary to reproduce, and press for improvements to common fisheries policy

- New sustainable shipping strategy

- Aim to raise consistent compliance with the European Bathing Waters Directive to at least 97% by 2005 and to achieve a significant improvement in compliance with its guideline standards

Indicators

Coastal and estuarine water quality

Inputs of contaminants into the sea

Compliance with Bathing Water Directive

Biodiversity in coastal/marine areas (to be developed)

Fish stocks around the UK fished within safe limits

State of the world's fisheries

agreements with developing countries are consistent with this aim. It will press for early ratification by the EU of the UN Agreement on Straddling and Highly Migratory Fish Stocks, which will bolster the role of regional fisheries organisations and emphasise the precautionary approach in managing fish stocks on the high seas. The UK will help West African Countries to implement the UN Food and Agriculture Organisation's Code of Conduct for Responsible Fisheries.

8.47 Knowledge of what sustainable fisheries management entails is incomplete. The Government is promoting research on management measures and on the impact of fishing on the marine environment.

MANAGING COASTAL AREAS

8.48 Many of the UK's coastal systems are subject to pressures such as urbanisation, recreation, agriculture and industrial activities. Sea level rise due to climate change will be a further factor in future. Integrated Coastal Zone Management (ICZM) is an approach to managing these pressures, usually involving local and regional authorities and other organisations producing a joint plan for a particular estuary or stretch of coast. These non-statutory plans cover issues such as recreation, conservation, flood and coastal defence, water quality, fisheries and landscape. The Government supports this approach and is closely involved in an EU Demonstration Programme on ICZM which expects to report in 1999.

Soil

8.49 Soil is an integral part of the environment. It is essential for the production of food and other crops, for maintaining biodiversity, for the landscape. It contains much archaeological evidence of our history.

8.50 Soil quality is not a major problem in the UK, although there are localised problems of erosion, acidification and other contamination. But there are long term pressures on soils. Minimising the loss of soils to new development presents a particular challenge. In the past, soil protection has received less attention than the protection of air and water. The Government will ensure that soil protection

receives equal priority in future. A draft soil strategy for England and Wales will be available for public consultation shortly. Taking forward strategies for Scotland and Northern Ireland will be the responsibility of the devolved administrations.

8.51 The strategy will identify pressures on soils and set out objectives and measures for soil protection and include indicators of progress. It will also set out action to improve understanding of soil processes and to increase public awareness of the importance of soils.

CONTAMINATED LAND

8.52 Land contamination can cause harm to human health and the wider environment, including pollution of water resources. To deal with cases where contamination is causing unacceptable risks, later this year the Government will bring into force a new regulatory regime[10] which will clarify local authority duties to identify problem sites and to require their remediation.

Key actions and commitments
• New soil strategy
• Action to raise public awareness of the importance of soils
• New regulatory regime to clarify land remediation duties

Indicators
Net loss of greenfield soils to development
Concentrations of organic matter in agricultural topsoils

10 Part IIA of the Environmental Protection Act 1990

Landscape and wildlife

8.53 The special natural, cultural and archaeological characteristics of our landscape are highly valued and must be retained. We must also reverse the decline in wildlife and habitats – our biodiversity.

8.54 Our aim should not be a landscape frozen in time. What we treasure today is the result of centuries of gradual change. The activities of our ancestors, in particular in agriculture, shaped the landscape; many landscape features are archaeological sites. Important wetland sites came from mineral workings. Many reservoirs provide valuable recreational and visual amenity. In urban areas, rich wildlife sites have grown up on land that was once derelict.

8.55 Some change is inevitable, allowing for activities such as local enterprise, agriculture, forestry and renewable energy production, or to meet housing needs. But change must be well-managed. The Government is undertaking 'Countryside Survey 2000', a national audit of habitats and landscape features to mark the Millennium. Its results will show how the British countryside has changed over the past ten years and will be used to help assess whether policies for a sustainable countryside are working. A parallel survey is taking place in Northern Ireland.

PROTECTING THE WIDER LANDSCAPE

8.56 The Government's approach to protecting the wider landscape includes:

- **Identifying what is important.** Countryside Survey 2000 will complement the Countryside Character initiative, developed by the Countryside Commission[11] and English Nature in association with English Heritage. That initiative looks at landscape and nature conservation features in the English countryside, and helps national and local policies to strengthen countryside character. The Countryside Council for Wales is developing a similar approach.

The government will promote public access and the enjoyment of the landscape

- **Special landscape designations,** such as National Parks and Areas of Outstanding Natural Beauty (AONBs), which protect the finest countryside. The Government is reviewing the protection, administration and funding of AONBs, as well as looking at possible changes to the particular arrangements for the New Forest and South Downs. New National Parks will be created in Scotland. In all cases conservation of natural heritage will be integrated with local needs for economic and social development.

- **Promoting public access and enjoyment of the landscape.** In England and Wales there will be a new statutory right of access to mountain, moor, heath, down and registered common land. The rights of way system will be improved. National Lottery Distributors will support access to the countryside through their programmes.

- **Agriculture and sensitive land management.** Agricultural policy is determined by the EU Common Agricultural Policy (CAP) (see para 6.60). This has been very successful at securing reliable food supplies but subsidies to farmers and the increased pace of technological change have led to unacceptable impacts on the environment. The Government will continue to provide grants and advice to farmers to encourage environmentally sensitive land management, promote biodiversity and protect soils, landscape and historic features.

11 Now the Countryside Agency.

- **Protection for individual features** such as hedges, ponds, drystone walls, and historic and archaeological sites. The Government will provide advice and incentives to support sound management of these features, and will strengthen legal protection of important countryside hedgerows in England and Wales. Following the Countryside Survey 2000, it will consider whether other field boundaries should be given legislative protection.

- **Local Heritage Initiative:** The Countryside Commission's Local Heritage Initiative is a national pilot project on how to help people record and care for their local landscape, landmarks and traditions. It is hoped a full scale initiative will be launched in 1999.

PROTECTING AND ENHANCING WILDLIFE

8.57 Wildlife protection has often focused on special reserves which contain habitats and species which must be maintained. But there is a risk that populations become smaller, fragmented and vulnerable to extinction. Their long-term survival, and overall enhancement of wildlife, depends on action in cities, towns and the countryside as a whole. This involves:

- **National action.** The UK's national Biodiversity Action Plan co-ordinates activity to conserve and enhance biodiversity. It is overseen by the UK Biodiversity Group, drawn from central and local government, official and voluntary conservation bodies, business, farming and land management. Action plans for over 400 priority species and 45 habitats will be in place by summer 1999 and their delivery will be a key to success. The Group is preparing a Biodiversity Millennium Report, for publication towards the end of 2000, on the progress of national and local policies and plans. A regional Biodiversity Strategy is also under development in Northern Ireland.

- **Local action and involvement.** There are over 100 Local Biodiversity Action Plans, which enable communities to identify wildlife which matters to them and to contribute to national

biodiversity targets. The Government will encourage this process and the integration of biodiversity into Local Agenda 21 plans. It will encourage business to take account of biodiversity in environmental management, to prepare corporate biodiversity action plans and to act as 'biodiversity champions', supporting work on habitats and species. The New Opportunities Fund's *Green Spaces and Sustainable Communities* initiative will assist communities to learn about and care for important habitats.

Populations of some woodland birds such as the song thrush have fallen by more than half since the mid 1970s

- **Helping people to appreciate wildlife.** We need to help everyone enjoy wildlife, especially near their homes. The UK has a strong voluntary conservation movement and a long tradition of voluntary scientific effort in the field of wildlife. The Government is encouraging development of the National Biodiversity Network to better bring together this effort.

- **Stronger protection for special sites.** Around a quarter of the most valuable natural sites in England – Sites of Special Scientific Interest (SSSIs) – are in unsatisfactory condition.[12] The Government has consulted on proposals to strengthen protection substantially. These include a strong presumption against destruction or damage of SSSIs by development, and measures to secure better management so that human activity, such as recreation and agriculture, can continue in ways compatible with maintaining the favourable condition of sites. The Government will ensure delivery of its obligations under the EU Birds and Habitats Directives and international agreements such as the Ramsar Convention on globally important wetlands.

- **Building concern for wildlife into wider policies.** The Government will continue to examine its policies and programmes, including management of the Government Estate, in the light of its biodiversity commitments and will encourage other sectors to do the same. The place of biodiversity in regional planning guidance in England is being strengthened. Planning policy guidance on nature conservation will be revised and in Scotland, new planning guidance on Natural Heritage will achieve similar objectives.

Key actions and commitments

- Improved public access to the countryside

- Stronger hedgerows protection, and consideration of legislative protection for other field boundaries

- Biodiversity action plans on over 400 species and 45 habitats in place by summer 1999

- Consultation held on proposals to substantially strengthen SSSIs

Indicators

Populations of wild birds (headline)

Landscape features – hedgerows, stonewalls and ponds

Extent and management of SSSIs

Access to the countryside (to be developed)

Biodiversity action plans

Native species at risk

Trends in plant diversity

Countryside quality (to be developed)

- **Building an international framework.** The UK will continue to play a major part in international implementation of the Convention on Biological Diversity, which aims to conserve life on earth, ensure its sustainable use, and achieve the equitable sharing of the resultant benefits. It underpins much of the action described above. The Government will help developing countries to fulfil their Convention obligations, through bilateral assistance and the Darwin Initiative grant scheme. Its 'Linking Policy and Practice in Biodiversity' Programme aims to clarify the links between poverty and biodiversity.

8.58 Measuring the success of policies for the countryside is not straightforward. The countryside is appreciated for its character, tranquillity and cultural values: these are difficult to measure, but the Government will seek to develop indicators which reflect these qualities. The headline indicator of wild birds provides a broad measure of the overall health of biodiversity.

Forests and woodlands

8.59 Forests, woodlands and trees enhance our landscape and are habitats for wildlife. They are places for leisure and recreation and are an economic resource for timber production, tourism, and local development and regeneration. The Government will publish a statement on its policy for sustainable forest management later this year.

8.60 The Government's approach is based on better management of existing woodlands, and continuing expansion of our woodland area. The approach includes:

- **Sustainable management of forests and woodlands.** The 1998 UK Forestry Standard sets criteria for sustainable forestry and indicators at national level and also within individual forests. The Government will continue to develop and refine the Standard and report on progress. The Government will also continue to survey the overall health of our trees and woodlands, and aims to prevent the spread of pests and diseases, including those which may become more of a threat as a result of climate change.

Sustainable Management

Indicators of Sustainable Forestry in the UK Forestry Standard relate to all four sustainable development objectives. They cover forest soil condition, water quality, water yield, water discharge patterns, net carbon sequestration, air pollution, timber production, other production, nature conservation, workforce skills and safety, rural development, access and recreation, quality of life for local people, increased awareness and participation, community involvement, other land uses, conservation of heritage features and landscape quality.

- **Protecting ancient and semi-natural woodlands**, which make up about a quarter of our woodland areas and are particularly valuable for biodiversity and as a part of the historic landscape. Their area has declined and become increasingly fragmented. The Government aims to halt these trends. It will review measures for the protection of this woodland and if necessary introduce new measures for giving them added protection. It also provides grants for new native woodlands.

- **New woodlands and forests.** Woodland covers around 10% of the UK. The Government intends to increase that. It will promote opportunities for forestry within the reform of the Common Agricultural Policy. Woodland expansion will be considered alongside other land uses, respecting landscape character and allowing for appropriate consultation and environmental assessment.

- **Sustainable timber production.** Timber from our woodlands is an important and a renewable resource. In the next 10-15 years the amount of timber produced from our forests will rise steeply as trees come to maturity. The Government will work with all parts of the timber supply chain to improve quality and get best value from this crop. It has increased research into crop and timber quality and is developing proposals to encourage forest owners, through grant schemes, to develop long term forest plans which meet economic, social and environmental objectives.

- **Benefits for urban and rural development.** In addition to employment in forestry, wood processing and haulage, our woodlands also support jobs in recreation, tourism and conservation, particularly in rural areas. The Government will promote forestry in and around towns and cities to improve the local environment and restore former industrial sites. The Land Regeneration Unit in the Forestry Commission promotes the planting of new woodlands on degraded and contaminated land on the fringes of towns.

- **An integrated approach.** Last year, the Government published an English Forestry Strategy that identified four key programmes: forestry for rural development; forestry for recreation, access and tourism; forestry for

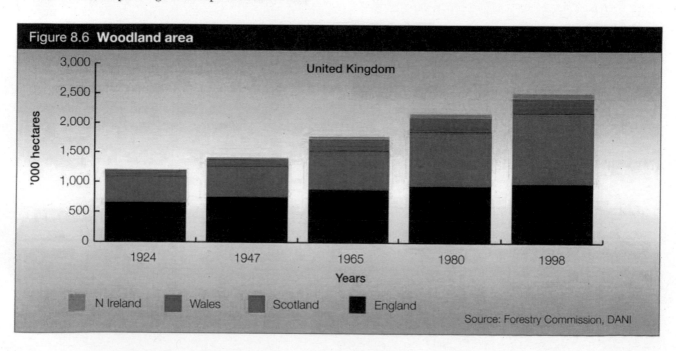

Figure 8.6 **Woodland area**

United Kingdom

'000 hectares

Years

N Ireland   Wales   Scotland   England

Source: Forestry Commission, DANI

economic regeneration; and forestry for environment and conservation. Under the devolved administrations, Scotland, Wales and Northern Ireland will set their own priorities.

- **Sustainable management overseas.** The Government works extensively with developing countries and multilateral organisations to promote sustainable forestry which helps local people to secure long-term benefits from their trees, and recognises the wider importance of forests for the world's environment. It also encourages the use of independent and voluntary certification and labelling schemes.

Key actions and commitments

- Policy statement on UK sustainable forest management to be published in 1999

- Future review of protection for ancient and semi-natural woodland

- Work with industry to improve value throughout the timber supply chain, through product innovation and market development

- Promote forestry in and around towns and cities through closer collaboration between regeneration, economic development and forestry interests

- Encourage the use of independent voluntary certification and labelling schemes through participation of Forest Enterprise and by assisting the development of a UK Woodland Assurance Scheme linked to the UK Forestry Standard

Indicators

Area of woodland in the UK

Ancient semi-natural woodland

Sustainable management of woodland (to be developed)

Number of countries with national forest programmes

Minerals

8.61 Minerals are a vital resource on which construction, manufacturing and energy industries depend. Aggregates dominate in tonnage and value but other minerals are also important, for instance:

- silica sand, fluorspar, potash, salt, and special clays in the glass, ceramics, electronics, chemical and fertiliser industries;

- cement raw materials, brick clay and gypsum for construction;

- deep-mined and opencast coal for energy.

8.62 The demand for minerals needs to be met as far as practicable at the least environmental cost and, as far as possible, without exporting environmental damage to other countries. This approach includes:

- **Location of mineral workings.** Resources of some minerals, notably aggregates, are extensive whilst others are more localised. Environmental and developmental constraints mean that not all resources can be worked. It is important to identify where extraction will have least effect on landscape, environment, and quality of life of local communities. Rigorous examination is given to proposals to extract minerals in National Parks and Areas of Outstanding Natural Beauty. Stronger guidance has been issued on the extraction of opencast coal in England and Scotland, and is in preparation in Wales.

- **Making the best use of minerals.** The Government aims to maximise efficient use of materials. It will work with the construction industry to develop a strategy for more sustainable construction, including targets for efficient use of primary aggregates and greater use of recycled and waste materials. It will encourage a reduction in the overall quantity of material used and in the generation of waste, and will help to make sure that higher quality materials are not used where lower quality materials are available. It will look towards more use of alternatives to land-won aggregates, such as marine sand and gravel, where these can be obtained in a sustainable way. Other approaches are also being developed. An aggregates tax will be introduced if the industry is unable to deliver an acceptably improved package of voluntary measures which address the significant environmental costs of aggregate extraction. The review of aggregates planning policy in England will re-examine targets for use of secondary and recycled aggregates, and the present method of providing for the future supply of primary aggregate.

- **Minimising impacts of extraction on the environment and local communities.** The Government is improving the regulatory framework which controls the impact of extraction. Consideration of the need for environmental impact assessment (EIA) is now mandatory for all significant proposals for new mineral workings, helping to ensure appropriate location of sites and sound planning conditions for the control of operations. Legislation will be introduced later in 1999 to extend EIA to offshore mineral dredging. Extended minerals planning guidance, to be issued from 1999 onwards, will advise on improving environmental management.

- **Rehabilitating sites to beneficial after-use.** Each mineral working should be restored to a standard suitable for a specific beneficial afteruse. Past reclamation was mainly to agriculture but there is now an increase in nature conservation and amenity uses: ways in which restoration can contribute to initiatives such as Biodiversity Action Plans are being considered.

- **Keeping planning conditions up to date.** The Environment Act 1995 included provisions for staged reviews of old minerals permissions. These reviews have begun. After the initial reviews, all existing permissions will be reviewed at intervals to help ensure that operational and restoration requirements meet the best current environmental standards. The Government will legislate shortly to apply European EIA requirements to these reviews.

Key actions and commitments

- Review of targets for use of secondary and recycled aggregates

- New minerals planning guidance to improve environmental management

- Review of policy on future provision for aggregates

Indicators

Amount of secondary/recycled aggregates used compared with virgin aggregates (to be developed)

Land covered by restoration and aftercare conditions

CHAPTER 9

International Co-operation and Development

To achieve sustainable development internationally we need to:

- work with others to eliminate global poverty and raise living standards in developing countries;

- work with others to tackle global pressures on the environment and resources;

- promote a fair and open trade system which respects the environment;

- strengthen the place of sustainable development in international organisations.

9.1   We live in an increasingly interdependent world. Sustainable development in the UK cannot be considered in isolation from sustainable development elsewhere. Our lifestyles have an impact on the rest of the world. We have a moral duty to help the poorest people in the world as we move towards a new global society. Allowing international inequalities to grow could jeopardise social stability and sustainable development for all of us.

9.2   Poverty and the environment are intimately linked, particularly in developing countries. Attempts to deal with one must address the other. Poor people are most vulnerable to environmental problems. They often have no choice but to use natural resources on which their futures depend. They need growth to escape poverty, but this must be based on the sustainable use of environmental resources.

9.3   This chapter covers three broad areas at the core of these issues: tackling global poverty and debt; strengthening the place of sustainable development within international organisations; and the links between trade and the environment. Chapter 8 showed how the UK action on global environmental and resource issues is reinforced by specific action to help developing countries. Chapter 6 considered the role of trade in improving the livelihoods of the poor overseas.

Tackling global poverty

9.4   About 1.3 billion people – nearly a quarter of the world's population – live in extreme poverty on less than US$1 a day. Almost 70% of them are women. Many more live in conditions which people in this country would regard as unacceptable. Their life expectancy is low, many of their children die before the age of five, many are illiterate, and they lack access to safe water and health services. More than a billion people live in inadequate shelter, without piped water, electricity, roads or security of tenure.

9.5   In May 1998, the *Human Development Report* from the United Nations Development Programme showed that while human development is improving overall, there are great inequalities between people and countries, between rich and poor, men and women and urban and rural communities. The 20% of the world's population who live in the richest countries have 82 times the income of the poorest 20%. Income disparities are also sharp within countries. Inequalities are not restricted to income but also cover health, education, opportunity and human security.

Across the world, 90% of people in urban areas have access to safe drinking water, but only 60% have in rural areas. National adult literacy rates range from 14% to 98%.

Education is important if we are to eliminate world poverty

9.6   The needs of the world's poor must become a priority. The Government endorses the Human Development Report's seven point agenda for action:

- raise consumption levels of the poorest;

- develop and apply environmentally sustainable technology;

- change taxes and subsidies to discourage environmentally destructive behaviour;

- improve consumer standards and education;

- strengthen international mechanisms to manage global impacts of consumption;

- build stronger alliances in civil society;

- think globally, act locally (including a crucial role for Local Agenda 21 programmes).

9.7   The 1997 White Paper, *Eliminating World Poverty: a Challenge for the 21st Century*, sets out the Government's strategy for eliminating world poverty, focusing on a series of internationally agreed targets for sustainable development.

International development targets

- reduce by one half the proportion of people living in extreme poverty by 2015;

- universal primary education in all countries by 2015;

- eliminate gender disparity in primary and secondary education by 2005;

- reduce mortality rates for children under 5 by two thirds, and reduce maternal mortality by three quarters, both by 2015;

- access through primary health care to reproductive health services for all by 2015;

- sustainable development strategies in all countries by 2002, and implementation in all countries by 2005;

- current trends in the loss of global and national environmental resources reversed by 2015.

9.8   To help achieve these goals, the Government builds partnerships with poorer countries, involving technical and financial assistance, policy dialogue with governments, and co-operation with other donors and multilateral development organisations. Government departments will work together to promote consistent polices towards poorer countries.

9.9   The Government seeks to reduce poverty through sustainable development. In the water sector, for example, the emphasis is on improving water supply and sanitation for poor people, reducing the heavy costs of ill-health and water carrying, and the long-term environmental and financial aspects of services. All programmes and projects financed by the Department for International Development are screened for social and environmental impacts.

9.10   The Government will continue to press for all countries to integrate poverty reduction and environmental concerns fully into economic policy at national and local levels. It will help individual countries to produce sustainable development strategies. As part of this, the Government is working with developing countries to help them define, implement and enforce appropriate environmental and labour standards. It will promote sustainable livelihoods for poor people, focusing on participation of local communities in planning and management, improving the access of poor people to land, resources and markets, and removing gender discrimination.

There is a market for sustainably produced goods from developing countries

9.11 Trade and investment are crucial to poverty elimination. They bring resources that can help generate the growth needed to establish sustainable livelihoods. The Government will work hard to ensure that the benefits which follow from the fall of barriers to international trade and investment reach the poorest people.

DEBT

9.12 Debt relief is a key element in meeting international development targets. The UK has cancelled debts on aid loans worth £1.2 billion and has encouraged other donors to follow our lead.

9.13 In March 1999, the Chancellor and the Secretary of State for International Development announced that the Government would be pressing for a new debt relief package in the run-up to the millennium. Their proposals, if agreed to by the

major countries, would involve a commitment by the end of 2000 to reduce the debt burden of the world's poorest countries by $50 billion. This reduction in the debts owed by developing countries would be achieved through a number of changes to the IMF/World Bank's Heavily Indebted Poor Countries (HIPC) initiative; raising the current ceiling on debt relief provided by the Paris Club of official creditors; and selling a proportion of IMF gold. The UK is pressing for the resources released from the debt repayments to be invested in poverty reduction.

Promoting sustainable development within international organisations

9.14 The Government will encourage international organisations to integrate sustainable development into all areas of their work. The UK spends half of its money on development programmes through international organisations, and will promote sustainable development principles in these programmes. For example, the Government will:

- continue to press for effective implementation of the European Commission's environmental assessment procedures and will work to ensure that its policies do not inadvertently undermine the interests of developing countries;

- work to ensure that the successor to the Lomé Convention – which provides a framework for EC aid to Africa, the Caribbean and the Pacific – has a strong poverty elimination focus and that its new trade arrangements help to integrate developing countries into the global economy;

- encourage the World Bank to apply stringent environmental and social assessment criteria to its projects, and to promote sustainable development through all of its activities;

- continue to play a significant role in the United Nations system, including through its Commission on Sustainable Development, whose overarching themes for the next five years are sustainable consumption and production, and poverty eradication;

- support initiatives to build sustainable development into the work of the Organisation for Economic Co-operation and Development (OECD).

Promoting sustainable development within the UK Overseas Territories

9.15 The Government is working with the governments of the UK Overseas Territories to achieve the common objective of managing sustainably their natural resources in ways which offer benefits to the local people. Our recent White Paper, *Partnership for Progress and Prosperity*,[1] makes clear that both the Government and the UK Overseas Territories will address environmental responsibilities consistently and systematically. Together, we shall develop an Environmental Charter to clarify the roles and responsibilities of various stakeholders, taking into account the wide variety of circumstances and local resources in each Territory.

Antarctica

For 40 years Antarctica has been managed by International Treaties. For the most part, this has proved an effective mechanism for protecting Antarctica's environment and managing its resources. But some problems remain. Some parties have not implemented it effectively and not all countries are members. One result is over-fishing of the Southern Ocean and wholesale slaughter of some sea birds. The UK will play its full part in international efforts to improve the enforcement of the Treaty system and to ensure that Antarctica remains a place of peace and security.

Trade and environment

9.16 National economies are becoming increasingly connected. A quarter of global output is traded between countries: trade flows have increased 17-fold in 50 years. Along with rapid technological developments, trade and foreign investment have been a driving force behind globalisation. Concerns have emerged about the implications of trade liberalisation and international competition on the quality of the environment.

9.17 The World Trade Organisation (WTO) provides a multilateral rules-based system which gives all countries the opportunity to participate in the global economy and seek redress on a fair and equal basis, based on non-discrimination, transparency and consensus. The international framework governing the environment builds on this approach and on the precautionary principle and the polluter pays principle. The Government believes that protecting the environment and maintaining an open, non-discriminatory and equitable multilateral trading system are equally important objectives. If the right frameworks are in place, both should be achievable.

9.18 Liberalising trade can help to ensure that resources are used efficiently, to generate the wealth necessary for environmental improvement, for development, for the spread of cleaner technology and for improved social conditions. On the other hand, where economic activity is unsustainable, trade can act to magnify this, increasing pollution and depletion of natural resources such as forests, fish and other wildlife, and minerals. Governments need policies to allow trade liberalisation to make its full contribution to sustainable development. The box below shows the principles the Government will follow in taking forward its policy on trade and the environment.

---

1 *Partnership for progress and prosperity: Britain and the Overseas Territories*. March 1999, Cm 4264. ISBN 0 10 142642 9.

Trade and environment principles

- Working closely with its European partners, the Government prefers to use the international framework to seek to influence the environmental policies of others, particularly through the development of multilateral environment agreements to tackle global problems. However, it does not rule out further action at European Union level if justified and consistent with the UK's international obligations.

- The Government affirms all governments' right to regulate for environmental improvement, provided that foreign imports and foreign investors are treated in the same way as comparable national products and companies.

- Domestic environmental regulation should not be used with the hidden aim of blocking other countries' trade. Nor should environmental priorities be cast aside when opening up markets or investment opportunities.

- The Government welcomes voluntary initiatives in the marketplace addressing the environmental effects of products (for example, voluntary labelling and related ethical trading initiatives), especially if they open markets for sustainably produced goods from developing countries.

- Environmental and trade policies should be developed in a framework of good governance and in an open and transparent way, without breach of international obligations and without adverse impact on the environment of others. Within that framework the Government recognises the rights of other governments to set different priorities on the environment according to their circumstances.

- Trade arrangements with developing countries should be used to promote sustainable development in developing countries in a way that does not discriminate against their exports.

- The Government believes action for the environment should be analytically based, taking into account scientific evidence, while acknowledging that this will not always provide full certainty. Risks need to be fully assessed, including the risks if action is not taken. The Government considers both the short and long term economic and social benefits and costs before taking decisions.

NEW TRADE NEGOTIATIONS

9.19 The Government supports greater incorporation of environmental concerns into trade policy, so that international frameworks for trade and the environment work in a complementary way. With its EU partners, it will aim to secure this through the new comprehensive trade negotiations which the EU wants to start in 2000. It will contribute to development of methodologies for assessing whether new trade agreements will benefit or damage the environment. It will discuss with EU partners and the European Commission the parameters of such assessments, and how to use them during trade negotiations.

9.20 The WTO Ministerial Conference in May 1998 highlighted the issue of transparency. There are two elements. First, the Government welcomes moves to make WTO more open: for example, wider release of documents, greater use of the Internet, and through events such as the recent High Level Symposia on trade and environment and trade and development. At the same time, the WTO must remain as a forum for negotiations between governments. Secondly, individual WTO members have a key role in communication at the national level, so that their approach to negotiations in the WTO reflects the balance of national interests. The Government is committed to the maximum possible openness and accountability in this regard.

MULTILATERAL ENVIRONMENT AGREEMENTS (MEAS)

9.21 There are many international conventions aimed at protecting the environment. Some have the specific purpose of imposing controls on trade, for example in endangered species; others include trade restrictions on substances harmful to the environment, such as ozone depleting substances. Restricting trade in such substances and species with non-members of an MEA has provided an effective enforcement measure, but trade controls should be used only to the extent necessary as part of an integrated policy package.

9.22 The UK believes, alongside our EU partners, that there is a need to clarify the interface between MEAs and multilateral trading rules. At present, uncertainty about the relationship between MEAs and WTO rules may inhibit the development and application of trade measures in MEAs, although there has never been a case disputing existing MEAs in the WTO. The interface between the two internationally recognised legal systems could be clarified by a political declaration, by an interpretative understanding of GATT Article XX, by amendment to existing WTO provisions, or by a new free-standing agreement on MEAs within the WTO. Progress in the WTO is dependent on consensus and is likely only as part of a wider trade negotiation, such as the expected forthcoming WTO Round. We will work to build agreement on the way ahead within the EU and internationally. We will also work to invigorate the provisions on compliance contained in key MEAs, such as CITES and the Convention on Migratory Species, to ensure that compliance and enforcement are given high priority at the Conferences of Parties to MEAs.

Measuring impacts

9.23 Rich and poor countries may have very different 'environmental footprints', which give a broad indication of their effect on the global environment. There is no single way to measure a 'footprint'. In terms of carbon dioxide emissions, the United Kingdom, with 1% of the world's population, emits 2% of global carbon dioxide. The United States emits twice as much per person, Ethiopia a hundred times less.

9.24 A uniquely environmental view of a 'footprint' may be too narrow. The Government will sponsor a seminar on the United Kingdom's 'sustainable development footprint', which will consider the social and economic benefits of trade and development, as well as environmental impacts.

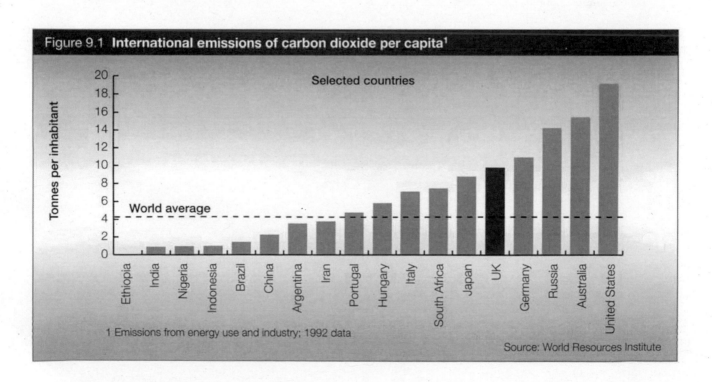

Figure 9.1 International emissions of carbon dioxide per capita[1]

Selected countries

Tonnes per inhabitant

World average

Ethiopia, India, Nigeria, Indonesia, Brazil, China, Argentina, Iran, Portugal, Hungary, Italy, South Africa, Japan, UK, Germany, Russia, Australia, United States

1 Emissions from energy use and industry; 1992 data

Source: World Resources Institute

Key actions and commitments

- Implementation of White Paper on eliminating world poverty

- Press for international organisations to take more account of sustainable development

- Reinforce efforts to incorporate environmental concerns in international trade policy

Indicators

Global population

Global poverty

Overseas development aid/bilateral aid to low income countries

UK public expenditure on global environmental protection

Implementation of multilateral environmental agreements

International emissions of carbon dioxide per capita

World and UK materials consumption levels per capita (to be developed)

CHAPTER 10

Action and Future Reporting

10.1 This Strategy sets the framework for action to deliver sustainable development in the UK. The challenge is great: to some it will seem daunting. But we can take heart from what has been achieved in the past. Forty years ago, only 5% of houses had central heating. Today, around 90% do. In the same period, the proportion of homes with no inside toilet has dropped from around 7% to a fraction of 1%. Fifty years ago, 32 babies in every thousand died within a year of being born, today the figure is only 6. Whereas today nearly 60% of 17 year olds are in full-time education, fifty years ago about 75% had left school by 15.

10.2 We have solved many of the pollution problems we once faced. Far fewer of our rivers are lifeless as a result of industrial effluent and sewage. The amount of sulphur dioxide created by our power stations, one cause of acid rain, has fallen by 55% in the last 25 years and is still being reduced rapidly.

10.3 In other respects we have been less successful. These are the sustainable development priorities for the future:

- more investment in people and equipment for a competitive economy;

- we need to reduce the level of social exclusion;

- promoting a transport system which provides choice, and also minimises environmental harm and reduces congestion;

- we need to make our larger towns and cities better places to live and work;

- directing development and promoting agricultural practices to protect and enhance the countryside and wildlife;

- improving energy efficiency and tackling waste;

- working with others to achieve sustainable development internationally.

10.4 As the economy grows, consumers will have more money to spend. Economic growth of around 2¼% – the average over the past 30 years – would mean that, by 2050, real incomes in the UK would be around three times their current levels. If that increased spending power is to be compatible with sustainable development, then:

- the products we buy must be more efficient than they are now in terms of the resources they use throughout their lifetime; and

- businesses will need to meet consumer demands with new kinds of goods and services which have a low environmental impact.

10.5 The challenge may seem daunting in terms of what has been achieved in the past. But for particular products, rapid progress has been made. Computer chips are halving in size and doubling in performance (that is, achieving a 'factor 4' improvement) every 18 months.

10.6 Part of what is needed to secure sustainable development is obvious. It is a matter of extending existing best practice and making good glaring shortcomings. For example, our housing is less energy-efficient than that of some European countries. Tackling that problem will not only reduce our emissions of carbon dioxide but will reduce heating bills and eliminate the scourge of fuel poverty. Elsewhere, the answers may be less clear. Integrated thinking is vital.

10.7 The principles we have identified will help us decide how to cope with new decisions we shall face – in particular how to weigh the benefits of innovation against the risks. We know that, in the future, we may need to redouble our search for new technology, or rediscover old approaches.

10.8 The task of achieving sustainable development is made easier by the toolkit we have assembled. The indicators are a vital part of this: they will tell us whether we are heading in the right direction. If we are not, then we shall need to look for new ways of meeting our objectives. We have too often given the wrong signals by failing to make people face the environmental and social costs of their actions. We shall need to use the full range of measures in future, but economic instruments will play a larger part than they have in the past.

10.9 Sustainable development requires the participation of everyone in the UK. So it is essential that we find better ways of involving all sectors, and the public at large, in decisions. The Government has sought to adopt an inclusive approach in the preparation of this Strategy, and will continue to do so.

FUTURE REPORTING ON SUSTAINABLE DEVELOPMENT

10.10 This Strategy has highlighted the increasing amount of reporting on sustainable development issues – including reporting by businesses, by local authorities and by individual Government Departments and public bodies. The Government welcomes this trend, which it will continue to encourage.

10.11 In addition to individual reports of this kind, there is a need for periodic reporting on progress by the country as a whole towards sustainable development. The Government therefore proposes to bring together and publish once a year the latest information about progress against each of the headline indicators, and to account for the action that the Government has taken, and proposes to take, in priority areas. It will publish this review annually, starting in 2000.

10.12 In due course, sustainable development priorities are likely to change. Some challenges will be met; new ones will emerge. We shall discover that we were more optimistic than was justified in some respects and more pessimistic in others. The annual reporting systems must be flexible enough to cope with this. The involvement of all stakeholders in a transparent reporting system will be a key tool in promoting the behavioural change that will allow progress to be made towards sustainable development. The Government envisages a full review of this Strategy after 5 years.

10.13 To promote the involvement of all sectors in sustainable development reporting, the Government proposes that a key element of the remit of the new Sustainable Development Commission (see paragraph 5.25) should be to monitor progress. This will include reviewing the state of sustainable development in the UK as revealed by the indicators; whether the action being taken by each sector is, in its view, sufficient; and if not, what more needs to be done.

10.14 The Government intends to hold a seminar in order to seek the views of all stakeholders on how a system for monitoring and reporting progress towards sustainable development can best be designed and implemented.

Printed in the UK for The Stationery Office Limited on behalf of the
Controller of Her Majesty's Stationery Office
Dd 5068822, 5/99, 39462, Job No J0081013